The Teddy Bear Catalog

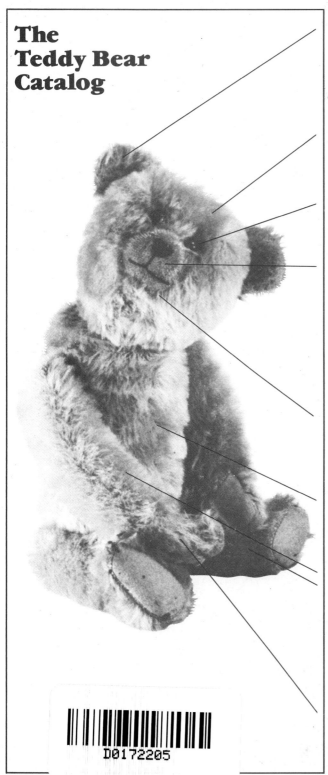

Ears: The most fragile of a Teddy Bear's appendages, ears are often subjected to rough treatment and misused as handles.

Brain: Teddy Bear brains are remarkable for remembering only good things.

Eyes: Shoe buttons, buttons, glass stickpins, plastic, and thread are often used as eyes.

Nose and Mouth: Many bears start out with embroidery thread noses and mouths that are eventually worn away after years of serious cuddling and snuggling.

Voice: A bear's voice does not determine its sex. Teddy Bears are asexual. A deep voice indicates a "growler," a high voice, a "squeaker."

Heart: While invisible, the heart encompasses the entire torso of the Teddy.

Arms and Legs: Jointed limbs are preferred. Joints prevent torn ligaments and breakage. They also make it easier for bears to wave out of car windows.

Paws: Even when seriously damaged they still retain the ability to hold the smallest hands.

The Teddy Bear Catalog

Prices,
Care and
Repair,
Lore,
100s of
Photos.
Everything.

Completely
Revised
and
Updated.

Peggy &
Alan
Bialosky

Workman
Publishing
New York

Cover Teddy Bear:

Bialosky Bear;
early 1900s;
100% loyal and true.

Library of Congress Cataloging in Publication Data

Bialosky, Peggy.
   The Teddy bear catalog.

    1. Teddy bears—Collectors and collecting—Catalogs.
1. Bialosky, Alan. II. Title.
NK8740.B5 1983   688.7'24   84-40040
ISBN 0-89480-607-6 (pbk.)

Cover Design: Paul Hanson
Cover Photograph: Jerry Darvin
Book Design: Florence Cassen Mayers with Lorraine Edminster
Illustrations: Susan Gaber
Photographs: Marvin M. Greene
Additional Photographs: Peggy and Alan Bialosky; Stephen Butler
Special thanks to the following for use of their photographs in *The
Teddy Bear Catalog: The Washington Post,* page 12 and 14;
Marguerite Steiff GmbH, (Margarete Steiff, page 17 and "Jackie," page
26; Ideal Toy Corporation, all photos page 16; R. Dakin & Co., Pandas,
page 23; Cecil St. Clair King, page 34; Kay Bransky, page 55; Terry L.
Michaud, "Gymnast Bear," page 62; Allan Teger, "Bruino," page 199.

Workman Publishing Company, Inc.
1 West 39 Street
New York, NY 10018

Manufactured in the United States of America
First printing of first edition October 1980
First printing of this edition January 1984

10 9 8 7 6 5 4 3 2 1

Dedication   To EDS: Whose fatherly appreciation of fine toys and fantasy included the gift of a childhood filled with Teddy Bears—and the belief that all stuffed animals are somehow quite real, and intended at least in our hearts, to last forever.

Acknowledgments   The authors gratefully and warmly thank and acknowledge the special people who helped with the research, stress, and preparation of our books. With deep appreciation, our most sincere gratitude goes to:

Marvin M. Greene; David, Jeff, Mary Ann, and Randy Bialosky, and:

Applause; Wallace Berrie & Company, Inc.; Tim and Nancy Atkins; Diane Babb, J. D. Babb, Inc.; Dorothy Bordeaux; Kay Bransky; Edson J. Brown and Ross Trump, Brown-Trump Farm; Stephen Butler; Virginia Caputo; Elsie Carper, *The Washington Post;* Karen and Kevin Carr; Susan Critchfield, *The Washington Post;* Donna Datre; Sylvan Engel; Billie and Lyle Fagan, Fagan International, Inc.; Gerald Fisher; Ed Freska; Pat Garthoeffner, Toy Box Antiques; Helen Greene; Tracy Greene; Gund, Inc.; Paul Hanson; Ideal Toy Corporation; Ruth Kalb; LaNore and Richard Kaplan; Emily St. Clair King; Knickerbocker Toy Co., Inc.; Terry and Ralph Kovel; Roland M. Kraus; Doris and Terry Michaud, Carrousel; the late B. F. Michtom; Janee Lutticken McKinney and Howard McKinney; Hilda Nieman; North American Bear Co.; Tim O'Brien; Bob and Jackie Olson; Jim Ownby; Jan Pitney; Don and Mary Jane Poley, Mary Jane's Dolls; Susan and Matt Procino; Suzanne Rafer; Herbert, Rita, and Bruce Raiffe; Kathy Goldblatt and Ruth Rashman, Rashman & Associates; Reeves International, Inc.; Harry Rinker; Zeke Rose, Porter, LaVay & Rose; Bonnie Rowlands; Dr. Mark Rutman; Beth Savino, Klee Sherwood; John Shook; Skine; Hans Otto Steiff, Marguerite Steiff GmbH; Rose Vargo; Barbara Wolters; Peter Workman and the entire staff of Workman Publishing Company.

Contents

The Teddy Bear Catalog

Teddy Bear Price Guide

Directory

A Teddy Bear Update

When *The Teddy Bear Catalog* was published in 1980, collecting Teddy Bears was already a growing hobby. Bear fanciers began coming out of the closet and showing the world what they had saved from their own childhoods: wonderful, unique, hidden–for–years Teddy Bears of all sorts, sizes, and mechanical abilities. Collecting these irresistible playthings has now become, at the very least, a frenzy.

In revising the *Catalog,* we have gathered the opinions of other collectors, dealers, and experts, not only in the United States but from many other countries as well. In addition, utilizing our own travels, experiences, and observations, we have updated this book to give readers a general idea as to the background and value of Teddy Bears today.

Prices have risen. Values listed here are to be used only as suggested guidelines and are based on market averages figured at the time this book was revised. Please note that bears with unique qualities or appeal have risen in price at a greater rate than their more ordinary cousins. Prices will vary, depending upon a Teddy Bear's size, condition, appeal, quality, and rarity. Where sets are shown, the price of a complete set will exceed that of the sum of the prices for the individual pieces.

While every effort has been made to be accurate, the authors and publishers are neither liable nor responsible in any way for errors in prices, information, or identification of the bears.

We sincerely hope you and your bears will enjoy this volume as much as we have enjoyed redoing it. It truly has been a labor of love, and we think you will be very excited with the wonderful new and old "treasures" we've included.

Paddington's "Aunt Lucy"
(See page 182)

The Teddy Bear Catalog

Even in the early 1900s, Teddy Bears accompanied children during photographic sessions.

Bear Beginnings

The actual "creation" is clouded in controversy. But, once upon a time (in 1902), one way or another, the Teddy Bear was born.

Teddy, to his friends

You see, it all started this way: President Theodore Roosevelt refused, while on a hunting trip, to shoot a captured bear. Many available accounts, including popular retellings of the story, report the bear was a cub who either went on to live: at the White House; at a Washington zoo; in a hotel with a handler; as a pet with relatives of the president; or as the mascot of the hunting camp, depending on which version of the story you read.

A few versions also state the bear wasn't a cub at all, but a weak, older bear.

Curious about the discrepancies, we began to do some research. It seemed important to get to the bottom of at least some of the mystery surrounding the Teddy's earliest beginnings. What we found out (with the help of *The Washington Post*) was like finding there is no Santa Claus, or Tooth Fairy, or Easter Bunny—because it appears there really was no cute little bear cub.

Another myth up in smoke or No, Virginia...

On Saturday, November 15, 1902, the hunting incident, as it actually happened, was related in a front-page story in the *Post,* with a Mississippi dateline. The report was headlined, "One Bear Bagged," and further read, "But It Did Not Fall A Trophy To President's Winchester."

The Washington Post story that ran on November 15, 1902, related the hunting incident that initiated the creation of the original American "Teddy's Bears."

The detailed story goes on to explain that part of the president's hunting party trailed, then came upon, a lean, black bear (about 235 pounds). The exhausted animal was followed by the hunting dogs to a water hole. Desperate, the bear turned on the dogs, and even though it was "too exhausted to put up much of a fight," it managed to grab one of the hounds by the neck and kill it.

As the cornered bear made a swipe at another of the dogs, one of the men in the hunting party "knocked the game over with a blow on the head," probably with a rifle. "Then he blew his horn that the quarry had been brought to bay." A messenger was sent to bring back the president. Meanwhile, the bear was roped and tied to a tree. When Roosevelt arrived at the scene and saw the bear tied that way, "he would neither shoot it nor permit it to be shot."

"Put it out of its misery," he is reported to have said to one of the men. Subsequently, the hunter "ended its [the bear's] life with his knife."

Summing up the incident, the *Post* read: "President Called After the Beast Had Been Lassoed, but Refused to Make an Unsportsmanlike Shot."

But this is not the end of the story. On the following day, November 16, 1902, the refusal to shoot the bear became immortalized. It was coupled to a political incident related to a political dispute between Mississippi and Louisiana, and depicted in a cartoon by Clifford Berryman.

On November 16, the cartoon appeared on the front page of the Sunday *Post* as part of a montage titled, "The Passing Show." It shows Roosevelt, gun before him with its butt resting by his right foot. His back is to a plain, unhappy, *full-grown bear* with a rope around its neck, and Roosevelt is gesturing that he refuses to shoot the animal. Written across the lower portion of the cartoon are the words: "Drawing the Line in Mississippi." The cartoon received immediate and overwhelming attention.

The Washington Post.

THE PASSING SHOW.

YALE DOWNED TIGERS

Princeton Men Were No Match for Old Eli's Sons.

averaged about 50 yards. There is no telling what the score would have been had Princeton been without the services of Dewitt. Where Princeton was supposed to excel, namely in the back field, she was lamentably weak, and not until near the close of the second half, when an almost entire new set of players had been put behind the line, did Princeton show any aggressive line bucking.

Princeton contested every inch of the ground, and she deserves great credit."

Capt. Davis, of Princeton, said: "Our team put up a plucky fight, but the best team won, and we do not wish to take any credit away from Yale. She gained most of her ground through out line, and her attack was consistent, but most of her gains were short. Our hope of scor

But this is not the cartoon people are familiar with today. The one most often reprinted also has a 1902 date to the right of the signature. If you look closely, you will notice that this cartoon shows a smaller bear which seems more cub-like and appears to be shaking with fright. If you study the drawing, you will also notice that the president's rifle is resting more toward his left foot. In the *Post* cartoon, the President has two visible pockets on his jacket; there is only one visible in the other. The "shivering cub" cartoon is usually credited to *The Washington Star* and when Berryman left the *Post* he did indeed work for the *Star*; but that was after 1902 (he joined the *Star* in 1907), so the *Post* cartoon has to be the one which first appeared in print. During his career with the *Star,* Berryman included his by then famous bear in many of his cartoons—perhaps with each new rendering, it became more and more cub-like.

Opposite page:
The original Clifford Berryman cartoon as it appeared in *The Washington Post,* November 16, 1902. Although it may be difficult to tell in reproduction, the bear in this version is not shivering and has an obstinate, rather than scared, look on its face.

The more familiar Berryman cartoon attributed to *The Evening Star.* The bear has definitely taken on a more cub-like appearance, from its cute, helpless face, down to its quivering little body.

Enter the Michtoms

The American Teddy Bear's creators, Rose and Morris Michtom.

Despite what is probably the true nature of the hunting incident, and the look of the bear in Berryman's first cartoon, they both really seem to have triggered the birth of America's favorite stuffed toy, because subsequently, back in Brooklyn, New York, another event was taking place. Aware of all the attention the hunting incident and the cartoon had attracted, Morris Michtom, a shopkeeper, displayed two toy bears in the window of his stationery and novelty store.

His wife, Rose Michtom, had made these bears: light-colored plush, stuffed with excelsior, and finished off with black shoe button eyes.

Looking at the two toy bears, Morris Michtom had a brilliant idea: he sought and received permission from President Roosevelt himself to call the new toys "Teddy's Bears."

An original 1903 Ideal Teddy Bear, one of which is in the Smithsonian in Washington, D.C.

The Michtoms' appealing plush bears became an overwhelming success. As they were sold, new ones were made, and by 1907 the demand was so great that the Michtoms moved their store to a loft as the Ideal Novelty and Toy Company.

Through the years, we were fortunate enough to have had many conversations with the late B.F. Michtom, son of Ideal's famous founders and at one time a chief of the company himself. "It is hard to determine manufacturers of Teddy Bears made from 1903 to 1910 or so, as brands were not stressed in those days," he told us. "But practically all bears made in this country from 1903 to 1906 were made by Ideal. Thereafter much competition set in, and probably no one alive now can identify exactly the manufacturer. Most bears were fully jointed: heads, arms, and legs turned. These were made mostly by either Ideal when domestically manufactured, or by Steiff when imported."

About the same time that the Teddy Bear was created in the United States, it was also born in Germany.

The Steiff Company there, known for its unusually fine-quality stuffed animals, also made a wonderful stuffed bear toy during this historic 1902–1903 period.

Actually, the company's first stuffed toys weren't bears at all, but little wool-felt pincushion-type elephants. These were the original creations of Margarete Steiff, born in Giengen in 1847. During her childhood she fell victim to polio, which left her legs paralyzed and weakened her right hand. She wished to be independent and capable of earning her own living, and overcame her handicap by learning

Steiff on the scene

Margarete Steiff pictured with one of her Teddy Bears.

to sew. She offered the stuffed elephants to the neighborhood children, who were delighted with them.

The little elephants were so popular that larger and different animals followed: a donkey, a horse, a pig, and even a camel.

It just so happened that Margarete's nephew, Richard Steiff, was an artist who had an interest in bears; he had spent time sketching brown bears in local zoos. Collaborating with his aunt, he influenced the development of a little jointed mohair bear toy. This new creation was exhibited at the 1903 Leipzig Fair in Germany.

Its debut there created no great stir until the last day of the fair: an American buyer noticed it, obviously had faith in it, and ordered several thousand of the little bears.

According to Steiff authorities, early Steiff bears were used as table decorations at the wedding festivities of President Roosevelt's daughter. Teddy Roosevelt was so enthusiastic about the bears, say the Steiff people, that the assemblage referred to them as Teddy-Bears.

At any rate, in 1903, a total of 12,000 of the items were made by the company; in 1907, that amount was 974,000.

Members of the classes of 1905–1907, pictured at their recent Teddy University class reunion. The three in the middle, of course, were on the football team.

The Steiff company was soon spoken of as the bear factory in Giengen, so the bear's head became the symbol used on all Steiff labels. The metal button in the ear was added as an additional trademark label during these years—and is still, of course, used today.

The Gund Workshop

Other companies have been notable in the Teddy Bear industry, among them Gund, Inc. In 1898 in Norwalk, Connecticut, Adolf Gund established a small workshop manufacturing stuffed toys, the first such manufacturer in the United States. As the business grew, it became a partnership with Jacob Swedlin in 1910, and the expanding company was later moved to New York City. Gund was the largest stuffed toy manufacturer in America in those years.

When Adolf Gund retired in 1922, Swedlin took over the company, and it is still prized today for its fine quality and creative designs. In 1983 an 85th anniversary bear was made and sold, as were other collectible Gund bears.

Bears on Everything

During the years that followed Teddy Bear development, innumerable Teddy Bear–related items appeared on the market:

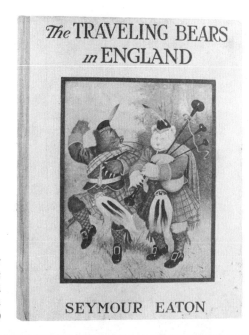

One of the early popular Roosevelt Bears adventure stories by Seymour Eaton (the pseudonym for Paul Piper.)

postcards, books (especially Teddy B and Teddy G: the Roosevelt Bears series written by Seymour Eaton, whose real name was Paul Piper), paper dolls, and bear dishes to use for children's tea parties, to name a few.

As the years passed, the Teddy Bear craze leveled off, but the Teddy Bear has remained a favorite toy, with millions sold yearly. Older bears and items related to them have now become collectors' treasures, and many of them are of extremely high value, both as nostalgic toys and in the amount of money they command. Some of the more unusual and appealing examples of this hobby are shown in the pages of this book.

An early photo of the author and her original bear friend. Separated sometime in her youth, the author has spent years of her life tying to relocate her bear. Pleads the author, "Teddy come home."

Bear Hunting

Want some advice on how to hunt down and buy a bear? If you are a beginning collector it is best to start by becoming familiar with and collecting new (modern) bears, for a number of reasons. New bears still wear their original tags and are bought from retail dealers. That means there is no great risk. You know exactly what you're getting: the name of the manufacturer, the stuffing and covering materials, and the name, if any, of the particular model.

New bears

Potentially collectible new bears of adequate quality frequently sell anywhere from ten dollars up, and are often in the fifteen to thirty-five dollar range. (High quality and prestige-brand bears may sell at higher prices). Since old Teddy Bears are far more costly, you can limit your financial risk by investing in a new one.

Furthermore, you can take your time selecting a new bear. Since other buyers aren't competing against you, you have time to think about the toy, knowing it will probably still be available the next day. Bears in limited editions or from closeout stock, of course, present a more pressured situation, but it is still not as competitive as the antique bear market. And buying from an established business means that if you decide the bear purchase is not really what you want or that it is defective, you can exchange or return it.

Making decisions

But which bear should you buy, and how do you select one? Generally it is best to pick a bear that is durable. If the arms and legs are jointed, is the bear made well enough so that those joints will not separate? Does the head swivel? Many youngsters try to turn the heads on their bears, and if that part of the anatomy is not jointed, the result can be, at the very least, a whiplash injury.

Keep in mind that many bears that are not jointed are still of fine quality. The important thing to look for is that it is not overstuffed, which puts too much stress on the seams. This can lead to frequent repairs and an unsatisfactory toy.

Once you have decided on the bear model, pick a cute face. Study all the expressions and choose one you really think has appeal. If you have to order by mail or phone, state on your order: "Please pick out one with a really appealing expression." Don't be embarrassed; after all, you're the one who is paying for it.

No matter how many identical bears a company makes, if you study a store display, you'll see no two look exactly alike. Some even have crooked eyes, pushed-in-noses, lopsided ears. Check the bear over carefully, and if you're not sure, don't buy anything.

Character bears

Many collectors become interested in character bears: Yogi Bear; Smokey the Bear; the Disney bears, to name a few. While characters are a separate category by themselves, they are still considered by most collectors to be versions of a Teddy Bear and are sought after as such. Pandas and Koalas are also purchased by some collectors, although a great many don't consider them Teddy Bears. Kissing cousins, maybe.

Some Teddy Bear collectors develop a passion for pandas even though they aren't Teddies.

Koalas in your Teddy collection? Why not?

One character acquired by collectors was Dakin's "Misha," which was originally tied in with the 1980 Moscow Olympics. Because there was controversy over the event itself and because the little stuffed bear's questionable fate was publicized, many people bought it as a relatively inexpensive gamble.

In its true form, Misha should be wearing its original detachable Olympic belt and original "Misha—Official Mascot of 1980 Olympic Games" tag. The Russian version, by the way, was jointed and fuzzier than American Misha by R. Dakin & Co.

Russian (jointed) "Misha" on the left and its U.S.–made counterpart by R. Dakin and Company.

Fozzie Bear, the Muppet, is an example of a collectible character with endearing qualities. For years, Winnie-the-Pooh, Paddington, and other childhood friends have been popular. Today, specific and creative characters are being made by many fine companies: North American Bear Company; Kenner; Gund, Inc.; Steiff; Merrythought Limited; Carrousel—the list could go on and on.

In addition to all this, there are now a growing number of extremely talented artist-bearmakers whose handmade Teddy Bears are unique, full of personality, and of wonderful quality—as you will see in the New Bears section beginning on page 174.

Today's marketplace offers buyers a wide range of future treasures in all shapes, sizes, fabrics, and price ranges. At no time in history could it be more exciting or rewarding to buy a bear!

This rare German Schuco yes-no panda is fully jointed with mohair fur.

Commemorative bears

Any bear tied in with a commemorative event is a good prospect for collectors. Steiff's two anniversary bears are naturals. Jackie is the bear Steiff put out in 1953, commemorating the fiftieth anniversary of its Teddy (first made in 1903). Originally it had a tag with the name "Jackie" and the fiftieth anniversary information, but these tags often fell off when children played with the toys.

Steiff's "Jackie."

Steiff's anniversary bear commemorating the company's 100th year.

The Steiff commemorative bear marking the company's 100th year is a reproduction of its first Teddy. It was available in a limited edition (11,000 worldwide: 5,000 with signed certificates in English, the balance in German) and originally sold for about $150. It now sells for $350 to $500 among collectors.

Steiff has put out other recent limited edition bears, including in 1981 a Mother-and-Baby (edition of 8,000); in 1982 a tea set birthday party with four bears (10,000), and a set of five white bears (4,200); in 1983 a "Richard Steiff" gray bear (20,000), a set of four brown Margaret Strong bears (3,500), and a set of three Teddy Roosevelt bears around a campfire (10,000).

Ideal has also produced special bears. Its 1978 Teddy Bear was the seventy-fifth birthday edition of its own original Teddy. Ideal also created a special "official" bear for the Good Bears of the World. (See the Directory at the back of this book under Clubs.)

Original Ideal Mascot for Good Bears of the World

The bear Ideal issued commemorating its Teddy Bear's 75th anniversary.

Premiums and foreign bears

Any bear that is very well made, particularly appealing, and a little bit different has a good chance of increasing in value. This includes bears offered as premiums, naturals for the beginning collector. Chase Manhattan Bank, Snow Crop, Travelodge, and Avon have offered attractive bears.

Foreign-made new bears are also desirable among collectors, even if they are regular line bears which are not produced for one special occasion. Austria's Berg; Switzerland's Felpa; France's Skine; Italy's Lenci; England's Merrythought, Dean's, and Nisbet; Germany's Hermann (as well as Steiff); and Käthe Kruse are but a few. Look around: you'll find more.

Party goers in 1907 enjoyed a bear game similar to Pin the Tail on the Donkey. This one has players feeding the berries to the bear.

Put a British bear on your shelf. These are two from Merrythought, one old (left), the other modern.

Check in the New Bear section of this catalog for photos of some bears which we believe will soon become collectibles. The directory beginning on page 212 gives company addresses if you would like to write for catalogs or other information. (Always include a stamped, self-addressed envelope.)

Antique bears

Now, let's go on to antique and other collectible bears. First, what are they? Purists feel antiques are one hundred years old or older, but most bear collectors don't adhere to that rule. How could they? The Teddy Bear was only born in the early 1900s.

Veteran bear hunters usually consider bears made before 1940 antiques. Bears made after that date but discontinued or changed in style may also become valuable and sought as collectibles. Both types are becoming difficult to find and expensive to buy. As more and more people are drawn to the magic of Teddy Bears, these items continue to increase in value. The best part of collecting them is that they exude their own special charm and charisma.

The long and the short of bear collecting.

Many collectors like to specialize. Some prefer Teddies that are six inches or under. Others buy only giants. Some bearaholics want the jointed types or mechanicals. Others insist their bears be covered only in mohair. Many collect bears produced by certain companies: Steiff, Merrythought, Chad Valley, Schuco, and Gund are among the more popular manufacturers of collectibles. Many people have enormous collections, sometimes three or four hundred bears. We know of one collection which contains 1,200. Don't let that throw you. A friend of ours has fewer than a dozen but they are of fine quality and in superb condition. Hers is one of the finest collections we've seen.

The hunt is on But where do you, as a collector, find rare bears? Flea markets, house sales, auctions, antique and doll repair shops, house or garage sales, basements or attics, resale shops—even trash cans. (Don't laugh! We've done it.)

A wonderful lady in England wrote us about an old bear her husband found lying in the middle of the street, possibly dropped from some passing car. Luckily for her, he rescued it, and it was a beauty. Lucky for that bear, too, of course.

Antique bears also show up at charity bazaars, rummage sales, and even in lost-and-found boxes at shopping centers, public stadiums, and arenas: anywhere lost mittens, boots and sweaters live. Scout around. Use your ingenuity; half the fun is in the searching.

Visit local stores that specialize in Teddy Bears and other antiques. Familiarize yourself with the feel and look of older bears. Find out as much as you can about the background of each bear from the retailer. Any information a knowledgeable retailer is willing to impart helps you in developing expertise in the field, and it will come in very handy when you are confronted with a labelless, seemingly unidentifiable flea market bear.

If you don't know of any stores to visit, consult the retailers list in the directory, beginning on page 216. Each listing includes an address and telephone number. If none are close by, write the retailers who are closest. Perhaps they know of other shops or private collectors near you.

Also consider joining a Teddy Bear club and subscribing to several hobby magazines and newsletters. These will keep you informed as to current prices, put you in touch with other collectors, and keep you posted as to current bear-related events. Check the directory, pages 221 and 224 for the names of clubs and publications.

The Teddy Bear Calendars are quickly becoming collector favorites. Shown here are the first three.

If you are having trouble finding old bears, try running a "Wanted To Buy" classifed advertisement in any newspaper or collectible-related magazine. Typical ads for this purpose might read as follows:

Try advertising

Wanted to buy—Old Teddy Bears in good condition from 1950 or earlier.

Or: Cash paid for Teddy Bears at least thirty years old. Related items also wanted.

(Related items can be clothes, dishes, prints, books, jewelry, almost anything.)

If you see a bear you feel is irresistible or that is part of a set of which you already own another part, buy it. Otherwise, if it is a rare bear or in good condition, by the time you think about it and come back it will have been long gone.

On the other hand, if you happen onto a bargain but don't really like the bear, it's not a bargain. Don't buy it. Learn to trust your instincts.

There are collectors who specialize in Teddy Bear postcards. This is an early example.

Bear alert What should you look for? The cream of the crop. Mohair, if you're lucky. Mohair was a term usually applied to material made from the hair of Angora goats, but these days the word often applies to fabric made of a wool and cotton blend. New mohair bears are expensive and often hard to find. To familiarize yourself with the material, you may have to learn on old bears. Again, an advanced collector or dealer might be willing to help. Although mohair can have either a soft or stiff feel to the touch, there is something distinctive and recognizable about it (its scent, for one thing).

Old Teddy Bears were stuffed with any of a variety of materials: straw (stiff and crackly, if you feel or squeeze a bear), excelsior (softer, pliable, sometimes crackly), kapok (softer, more huggable), wood-wool (firm). Kapok was also used for stuffing mattresses. It comes from the seed pods of trees that are sometimes referred to as silk-cotton trees. Wood-wool was a type of wood fiber that was processed to resemble wool. Some fine old bears have been filled with sawdust or even cork stuffing; others have cotton insides.

Before you go bearhunting, study pictures: old and new photographs, old prints, children's book illustrations, old magazine covers and illustrations. (Jessie Wilcox Smith and Bessie Pease Gutmann were two artists who used Teddy Bears as subjects.)

When bear hunters search for related items, plates like this one are what they seek out.

Examine your find

Often a well-loved, and by now collectible, Teddy Bear has needed emergency repairs during its lifetime. Replacement paws will not greatly alter the value of an old bear, if they are a close match in color and texture, and if they are neatly done.

Replacement eyes are common and do not alter the value at all, if the replacements are still genuine old eyes. Shoe button and stickpin eyes often fell out or were removed by wise parents for safety reasons. These items can still be found in shops and at flea markets. They are good to buy and put away in case you need a set of authentic eyes at a later date. Plastic buttons and eyes should not be used on antique bears. They give a grotesque appearance to the Teddy.

If an arm or leg has been replaced, the Teddy is not considered to be in "mint" condition (close to perfect), especially if the part has been made of new fabric. The value, therefore, is less. How much less is entirely up to the purchaser, who should keep the replacement part in mind. At least a third off the standard value seems fair.

Clothes don't necessarily make the bear

If the bear being sold is wearing clothes, have the seller remove them before you buy. Clothes sometimes conceal a major flaw. We bought a bear that was wearing a white dress; one arm appeared to be longer than the other, but the dealer assured us it was our imagination. When we got home and removed the garment, not only were the arms unmatched, but the paws themselves were different shapes and sizes. Take advantage of our mistake.

By the way, if a bear is dressed up, be aware that the clothes may have been added by other than the original manufacturer; judge the price accordingly. You can always find clothes later, so don't be afraid to buy a bare bear.

This jointed old mohair fellow is splendidly dressed in a handmade plush coat with brass buttons, and a cap with a visor made from an old leather wallet. He carries a parasol made from a dress belonging to the owner's great grandmother. This is surely Teddy Bear haute couture.

The better antiques, for the most part, are jointed at the shoulders and have swivel heads. Remember though: man-made fibers and plastic eyes and noses are all part of the modern world. Don't let anyone sell you a bear with a plastic nose or nylon plush and represent it as seventy years old.

Internal squeakers, growlers and musical mechanisms may have been removed or put out of commission through the years. Sellers will tell you that this doesn't alter the value of the bear, and if everything else fills the bill—and the bear is in good condition—you will probably pay about the same price as you would if the mechanism were working.

Beware of special toys like wind-ups, bellows music boxes, mechanicals, and any other perishable bears. Once the gadgetry stops working in these, you're in trouble—especially if you paid a high price because the toy was in working condition. Don't buy this kind of toy unless it's something that really appeals to you. You would be taking a risk.

Look out for reproductions and fakes when searching for antique bears. For example, there is a small jointed bear, originally made in Poland and distributed in the 1970s as a cute novelty, that has shown up at antique shows minus its label and with its plush dusty, and looking aged. At five or ten dollars the bear is still a cute novelty, but some antique dealers display it with a price of thirty-five dollars or more.

The guidelines in the price guide section of this book are suggestions. If you wish to study prices on your own, it is important to read three or four national publications to see how the market is going. The directory section has a listing of a few newspaper and magazine titles.

A quick word about prices

Go to at least three (and preferably more) antique shows. Be at the head of the line before the show opens. If good bears are for sale, they are frequently sold in the first few

minutes after the opening. Therefore, the early bird gets a chance to take a look before they're gone.

Friendly dealers have told us that when checking a garage or house sale ad, you should avoid going to those advertised as multi-family sales. If more than one or two families hold a sale together, you can be reasonably sure one of those insiders will buy any really good bears before the sale ever opens, making your visit a waste of time.

All this might seem like a lot of additional work, but in the long run it will save you aggravation and disappointment. When all is said and done, lots of people still make mistakes. One experienced antique collector bought an expensive Steiff Teddy which was supposedly over a hundred years old. At the time of purchase, she had forgotten there were no Teddy Bears before 1902.

Opposite page: You-must-have-been-a-beautiful-baby Bear looks comfortable in this buggy. Often you can find old carriages at flea markets.

Speaking of Steiff

Know your Steiff products before you buy a Steiff antique. The main identifying mark is a small metal button with the name Steiff impressed into it. The button is inserted into the left ear by the company. However, buttons are now appearing with increasing frequency in the ears of old bears which are *not* Steiff products—particularly at antique shows and flea markets. Therefore there is some risk involved when you purchase such a bear. (As you become more familiar with antique bears, the risk will lessen.)

Some early Steiff buttons (1907 and earlier) had no mark on the surface. Steiff buttons from approximately the same period have also been seen with a line drawing of an elephant impressed into the metal; both types can be considered rare.

Bear Care and Repair

Whether you own a collection of the most expensive antique bears or just a few that are brand new with future collectible potential, it is important to keep them in good condition.

A Teddy can still be a working bear—a toy that is played with, a mascot sitting on a bed or shelf, a traveling companion or a rear view mirror gymnast. Bear care does not require retirement from these duties.

New bears   If a new bear is stored in a closed cabinet, it remains relatively maintenance-free. Just vacuum it lightly every few months with a light weight portable vacuum cleaner (avoid heavy-duty power vacuums). If, however, it's stored where it gathers more dust, vacuum more frequently.

A bear that is frequently played with as a child's toy will need periodic baths. When the bear is tagged with its own cleaning instructions, follow them. Snip off the tag and save it in a safe, handy place. As a matter of fact, if you have a new bear you really like and want to save, take a photograph of it. Put the photo with any instruction tags (including the original price paid for the bear and the date purchased), and save all that material together. Should it ever become a collectible, everything can be put back in its original place, and you'll have additional background information as well.

Seam and rip repair   Before bathing, go over the Teddy, checking for split seams or other minor damage. Poke the stuffing back in with the blunt end of a crochet hook. Find thread that matches the fabric as closely as possible, and sew the rip closed with small, close-together stitches (see facing page). Underarm and neck areas (especially around what would be the collarbones if Teddy Bears had them) usually show the strain first, so check there for damage.

Replacement eyes and tongues (red felt) can usually be found at quality craft stores: buy extra eyes and keep them in your "bear kit" so you'll have them when you need them. (When a child's favorite Teddy Bear is unexpectedly injured, it sometimes requires prompt skilled emergency surgery if you want to keep peace in the house.)

By writing the manufacturer and sending the bear model number from the tags you saved, you may sometimes get exact matches in replacement parts.

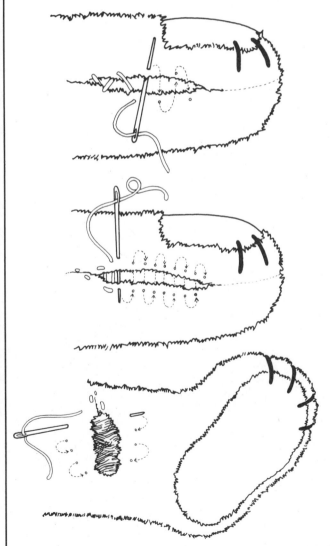

Ladder Stitch: Using thread that closely matches the color of the bear's fur, weave into and out of the fur as illustrated. Stay as close to the edge of the opening as possible, making sure to poke in any leaking stuffing with the blunt end of a crochet hook.

Lacing Stitch: This, too, will hold the fur of the Teddy Bear firmly together. Follow the illustration being sure to enter the fur from the wrong side and to exit through the right side.

If the Teddy Bear is ripped and the fur around the rip is very worn, use the ladder stitch, leaving as much as an inch of fur between the rip and the stitch. Tuck the worn fur under as you sew, easing it into the seam with the blunt end of a crochet hook.

Bathing your bear

Once you've given the bear a routine checkup, you can proceed with the bath. First, one caution that applies to all bears, old or new: what works for one person and bear might not work for others. There are differences in detergents, water, and touch. All caring and repairing instructions given here are suggestions that are based on what has worked best for us through the years. Anytime you work on a Teddy bear, some risk is involved. If you do damage a bear, don't let it throw you. Try to figure out what went wrong, and develop a safer way to perform the task. An injured bear is still lovable. Teddy Bears may fade, sag, stain or shed, but their personalities are never affected. They just go on being perfect.

Meanwhile, back to that bath. First, vacuum the bear. Spots may be treated with laundry stain removers which are available in supermarkets. but be cautious. Check for colorfastness in an obscure spot like the back of a leg or the bear's bottom before proceeding elsewhere.

To shampoo the bear, place it on a table which has been covered with a clean terrycloth towel. Take a small pan of warm water and add approximately one-eighth capful of mild liquid detergent. Stir it to a sudsy froth with a fork. Use a new

Teddy surrounded by some of the equipment needed to keep it in top shape. On the left: a self-standing blow dryer; basin; soft bristle brushes; metal dog comb.

long-handled brush with soft bristles like those used to clean Teflon. Before brushing any liquid onto a bear, always lightly shake your brush in order to remove any excess and avoid waterlogging. Then, beginning with the head, brush on the suds, using over-lapping clockwise light strokes. Keep cleaning the brush between applications by rinsing it in clear (preferably running) water and shaking it out.

After the bear has been lightly coated, take a clean washcloth, dip it in clear water, wring it out and damply (no soaking, please) wipe off the suds with light clockwise movements. As the cloth becomes soapy or soiled, use a new one or rinse the soapy one *thoroughly* before reapplying the cloth to the bear.

If you wish, you may add a second rinse by brushing on, with the same type of long-handled brush, a mixture of one-quarter capful of fabric softener diluted in a bowl of clean warm water. Rinse the brush in clear water before dipping it into the bowl again.

Timesavers

By the way, there are three quick methods of applying cleaning solution to new bears. You can try a spray bottle like the ones used for plants. Put some of the detergent-and-water mixture in the bottle, shake well and adjust to fine spray. Lightly coat the bear, then gently scrub off the soap using a clean damp cloth and overlapping clockwise motions.

Some people use pump-bottles of bathroom cleaner as the initial detergent. If you want to try this method, you should check your bear for colorfastness and fabric strength first. Use an inconspicuous part of the bear for a testing spot.

The third method is a good cleaning shortcut even for old bears. After vacuuming, apply a color-safe carpet cleaner onto the fabric. Brush it lightly with a damp brush which you may have to moisten several times. Let it dry for twenty-four hours and then vacuum again.

Fresh air and sunshine No matter which method you choose, once the bear is rinsed, put it outside on a clean towel and let it dry in the sun if possible. Also, if you brush certain bears lightly while they are drying in outdoor breezes and sun, they fluff up. Try the softer side of a nail brush.

One word of warning, new bear owners: some fabrics fade when left in the sun for too long. Don't plunk your bear in a sunny window and forget about it. A few hours of sun is plenty.

Some new bears may be machine-washed and/or dried in a clothes dryer. If you're using a dryer, put two or three dry bath towels in the machine, which should then be turned on for a few minutes before adding the bear. Always watch the drying time and temperature or you'll end up with a baked bear. Delicate fabric settings are the safest.

Once the bear is as good as new, clean all the equipment thoroughly and put it away in a box so you won't have to waste time regathering utensils the next time you're in the mood for bear washing.

Antique bears While some people leave venerable old bears in their darkened, matted condition, they look a lot better when they have been cleaned. Honest!

First, assemble the right equipment. Start with two small bowls, two long-handled, soft-bristle dishwashing brushes, two or three metal dog combs with variations in the set of the teeth, several terrycloth washcloths and towels, and at least one strong-powered hair dryer. We have found that two free-standing dog dryers (ours are made by Oster) work the best, because they blow the mohair fibers from different directions.

When you first bring home a very old bear, check it carefully for insects. Do not take any chances. Some bears, stored for long periods in basements or attics, have yielded silverfish, moths, spiders, and a few other unwelcome parasites. It pays to be careful. Suspected

A bear, from the early
1900s, was a $5 house-sale
purchase.

Antique jet beads were
added for eyes; the body
was restuffed, which also
restored the hump in back
and enabled the head to
remain upright.

New arm, ears (velvet),
and paws (felt) were
added, plus a new suit ($5)
and Teddy Roosevelt pin
(an antique retrieved from
the owner's jewelry box).
Completed bear in this
final condition might
bring $100 or more.

bears should be placed in an appropriate isolation box, along with mothballs or solid-stick insecticide. Most discount stores carry them. The box should be securely closed and left for forty-eight hours or so. This will result in the survival of the Teddy but the departure of any extra little guests.

Making do Take a portable vacuum and carefully go over the bear. Check the seams as you go. If any are ripped, sew them with thread that matches as closely as possible (see page 39). In order to keep the bear as authentic as you can, use old thread you or your friends or relatives may have. If stuffing has leaked out, it must be replaced before you close the seams. Straw or excelsior can be found in old stuffed animals too far gone to save. They are easily obtained at garage and rummage sales at a very minimal expense (say fifty cents).

Remove the filler material from these and save it. At the same time, if they have glass stickpin eyes, retrieve them. These will come in handy when you find sightless bears who need fast, authentic transplants. Other stickpin eye donors may be stone-marten boas (you know, those little ferret-like things that sneer at you from flea market tables). These taxidermy eyes suit smaller antique bears very nicely.

If you are unable to find any of the correct materials, don't be discouraged. For stuffing you can cut up clean pantyhose or stockings (but discard the elastic bands) into very small scraps. This will fill sagging bear parts, and at the same time dry quickly after cleaning. Even if it is a modern replacement, it's a pleasure to work with such material—and it's a great use for torn, unwearable stockings.

Pack the stuffing in *gently* with the blunt end of a crochet hook or the eraser end of a pencil—although the latter may be a little too thick. Unclog any internal packs of straw so you can intertwine the new filler with what's already inside. Never overstuff, because it puts too much strain on the aging fabric.

When you repair a rip in an old bear, sometimes the affected fabric is already frayed. You will have to discreetly stitch the fabric (from underneath) in areas as far away as an inch or so to make sure the repair will hold without further damaging the fabric (see page 39). If a ridge forms around the rip, gently push in the fabric ends so they don't show. By diverting the repair to a more stable area, you are spreading the stress and saving the bear from potential tragedy. Do nothing about missing or torn paw pads at this point.

This is the time to start the cleaning. Some owners use commercial dry cleaners on old bears and have been delighted with the outcome. The cleaners we interviewed, however, solemnly warn, "We will not guarantee anything, and this is done at your own risk." That's somber enough to scare us away. Besides, who wants to leave a Teddy Bear overnight in a dry cleaners without anyone around to reassure it or hold its paw?

This muff was renovated by removing a damaged doll's head and replacing it with a mohair Teddy Bear head: accomplished without damaging the swivel. A little creativity makes a one-of-a-kind piece, probably now worth about $85.

Old bears need baths, too

We prefer cleaning antique bears at home. The process is similar to the washing instructions for new bears but it is slightly risky and should be done more slowly and delicately.

If the bear has stickpin eyes, remove them and stick them into a bar of soap. This will allow you to clean the mohair head thoroughly and the eyes will be easier to reinsert later.

After the bear has been thoroughly vacuumed, spread a large clean towel over a table and place the bear on it. Follow the instructions for bathing that appear on page 40. For some older bears, when we feel it is really needed, we also add a little liquid chlorine bleach to this mixture, with very good results. Don't try this until you're experienced, however, because of the risk.

Keep a second bowl filled with clear warm water. Once the head has been soaped, take the second brush and, using only clear water from the second bowl, repeat the process to rinse off the soapy residue. A clean, damp washcloth can also be used for this stage. Be careful not to disturb the nose-and-mouth stitching.

As a final step, rinse one more time by dipping the clean brush into a clean bowl of warm water to which ¼ - to ½ - capful of fabric softener (preferably the kind with bluing) has been added and thoroughly mixed. Brush this on (light circular strokes), further removing any soap from the fabric. Again, keep the brush clean between applications by running it through clear water and shaking off the excess. Remember, never let the bear get too wet, and keep in mind that when it's damp, if you hold the animal too firmly, you will shift the stuffing.

After the head has been completely washed, do the torso, then the limbs. Skip the paws, keeping them as dry as possible if they are felt or any other fabric that might be damaged by water. Also, avoid the digit stitching where the arms join the felt of the paws.

When the whole bear has been completed, place it on a thick towel. Turn on the dryer and, beginning with the head, carefully, gently, cautiously, insert the comb at the base of the matted mohair (or other fur fiber). Lift it, fluffing it with the dryer as you work in order to restore the pile. Never let a hot dryer get too close to the bear; take your time while you work.

Now repeat the whole process on the torso; after that do the limbs.

During this comb-and-dry process, be careful not to rip the fabric with the comb. Be sure the metal teeth are not too sharp. (You can dull them with a file or Moto-Tool, if you have to.) Vary the combs, starting with wider-spaced teeth if there is a great deal of pressed-down matting. Facial fur is especially well restored if it is finished off with a fine-tooth "flea" comb (available at pet shops).

When the entire bear has been combed, it will still be damp. Place it on a dry white towel outdoors, if possible, or suspend it from a clothesline using nylon fishing line (tied loosely around the waist, not the neck). Warm sun and breezes, plus occasional fluff-up combing by you, will do the rest. Meanwhile, dip the glass part of the eyes in ammonia, then rinse, dry, and replace in the bear.

If it's winter, and you have heat registers, forced air heat will help complete the process. Fold a clean towel about ten inches from a register and seat the bear on that. From time to time, using the outdoor or indoor drying method, turn and refluff the animal.

Paw repair

As soon as it is dry, finish the bear by replacing any of the paw felt you feel is unsatisfactory. Search the usual antique haunts for old felt hats, coat or purse linings. If you can't find any authentic paw materials, buy new felt in as close a matching fabric as possible. See page 48 for illustrated instructions on replacing paw felt.

Using the shape illustrated, cut a piece of felt or other fabric ¼-to ½-inch larger on all sides than the size needed. One-quarter-to ½-inch in from the edge, make a dotted line around the fabric. Snip out tiny V-shapes from the edge of the fabric to the line, evenly spaced around the entire piece.

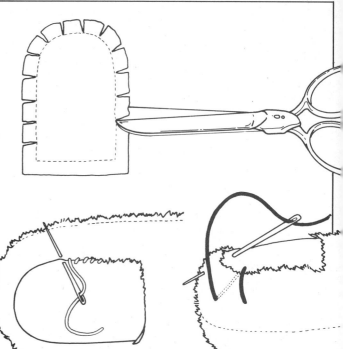

Iron under the snipped edge. Using matching thread strong enough to hold the felt to the bear's fur, make a knot in the thread end and sew into the paw. The knot should fall on the wrong side of the felt.

Place the paw fabric over the old paw fabric or where the old fabric originally was. Sew it down using tiny stitches, as illustrated. Bring some of the bear's fur up over the paw fabric to hide the stitches.

To make digits on the paw, use thick black upholstery thread and sew as illustrated. The knot on the thread should be hidden by the bear's fur. If not, gently push it beneath the fabric and into the stuffing.

Replacing a button eye

For example. If you need shoe button eyes and can't find any the right size and shape, color round beads with a black marking pen, then dip them in colorless nail polish. Beads from an old necklace often have metal loops which can be straightened with needlenose pliers to become stickpins—perfect for eyes.

Or if the bear is missing an eye and you can't find a replacement, make an eye patch, and your bear will look swashbuckling. If it is missing a paw or an arm, make a plaster cast and tell folks the arm was broken in a skiing accident.

Slip a long, strong length of thread through the loop or holes in the back of the button, drawing the thread ends even. Make a knot near the button end, and thread both lengths through a large-eye darning needle. Sew the eye to the bear as illustrated, making sure to place it even with the other eye. Bring the needle out behind the ear of the bear.

Pull the thread tight so the eye is flush against the bear's head. Slip the needle off and knot the ends of the thread together, close to the bear's head. Snip off the ends. The knot should be hidden by the fur.

Replacing an ear

If the bear's ear has fallen off, pin it as illustrated, and using small stitches, sew it to the head. For extra firmness, sew it to the head along the back edge, also.

Nose and mouth repair

With light-weight thread, make a nose and mouth shape using small running stitches as illustrated by the dotted line. The size of the nose and mouth is determined by the size of the Teddy Bear. Fill in the shape with embroidery thread, using stitches that are close together.

Making one neat stitch across, finish off the top of the nose shape. Use one stitch apiece to make the line down from the nose and each side of the mouth. If any of the knots in the thread are not hidden by the fur, ease them under the stitches so they don't show.

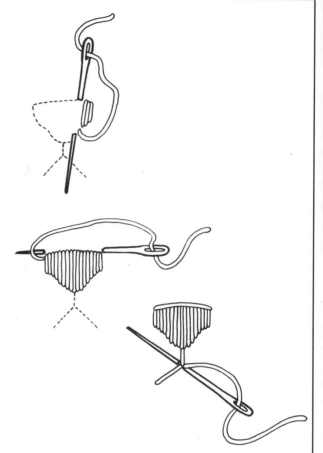

Calling in a doctor We did a plaster cast repair with a veterinarian, Dr. Mark A. Rutman of Chesterland, Ohio. We liked the way it turned out and asked the good doctor to write down the "prescription" in case you needed the brand names.

"The bear is laid on its side with the affected limb uppermost. Stirrups of one-inch diameter medical adhesive tape (Zonas Porous Tape, Johnson & Johnson) are applied to the end of the limb to prevent the cast from slipping. An orthopedic stockinette (Abco Products) is pulled over the limb to prevent the cast material from sticking to the fur. To prevent the cast from being applied too tightly, cotton padding (Cast Padding, Johnson & Johnson) is wrapped around the stockinette.

"A large bowl of cool water is prepared. A roll of two-inch plaster cast material (Extra Fast Setting Plaster of Paris Cast, Two Inch Rolls, Johnson & Johnson) is submerged in the water for several seconds. The excess water is then squeezed from the material with some care being taken to prevent too much of the plaster material from falling off into the bowl.

"The application of the cast is begun at the lower end of the limb and encircles it with each layer overlapping the previous layer by fifty percent. If needed, a second layer of cast material is applied over the first in a similar manner. The bear should be kept immobilized until the cast has dried completely, usually about fifteen minutes."

A cast can be used permanently or as a temporary aid until you can make the correct repair.

When we brought this bear home it was missing a paw and leaking stuffing from its wound. We had a veterinarian show us how to apply a real cast and were so pleased with the result that we almost kept it on for good. Eventually we rebuilt the missing paw and fixed the leak.

Teddy Bear Price Guide

French Mechanical
8 inches;
1880; French; clockwork
"Martin"; wind-up; very
rare.
$1,200

Pricing Bears

This section has been put together to show you approximate contemporary market prices of old, or discontinued modern, collectible bears. We have attempted to include bears in all price ranges, so that beginning collectors can try their luck knowing what to look for in their price range, while advanced collectors, more willing to spend greater amounts of money, can better identify real treasures and know their approximate monetary value.

Prices were carefully researched for years over a geographically large area by a study of antique shows, auctions, flea markets, individual collectors, manufacturers, and printed advertising prices in newspapers and magazines. Keep in mind that prices on individual bears depend upon age, rarity (Were there only a few made?), appeal (Is it irresistible?), quality, uniqueness (Was it a commemorative issue; a special occasion design; a specific character), and the general market for that particular bear.

In the text related to the photographs, all clothes were added after the bear left the manufacturer or retailer, unless you see the phrase "original clothes."

Also keep in mind: stuffings vary. Sometimes even very early owners changed stuffing when washing or repairing old bears. In addition, more than one type of stuffing was used in some bears. A bear stuffed with straw, for instance, may have had a kapok or wood-wool torso. During our years of snooping around (and into) bears, we've run into all sorts of stuffings: cotton, rag filler, tiny cork pieces, strips of rolled paper, sawdust, shredded foam rubber, wool, straw, excelsior, and all sorts of man-made materials. The stuffing mentioned with specific photographs is the primary material used in that particular bear.

Because so many collectors think of old bears as being straw stuffed, and have referred to

Be sure to dress your Teddy Bears in suitable clothing. This flea market find told us she was really Scarlett O'Hara so we dressed her in an outfit that would win the heart of any Rhett Butler.

them as such for so many years, bears that feel crackly to the touch will be referred to in this price guide as straw stuffed. You may wish to keep in mind that the crackly feel may mean the bear is not stuffed with straw but with excelsior. (Straw usually refers to dry stems or stalks of grain, while excelsior is made of long thin wood shavings.) The price value of straw- or excelsior-filled bears should be the same.

This price guide is to be used as a reference as well as a guideline. The prices listed are, unless otherwise designated, for bears in mint (or near-mint) condition. That means that if you're trying to sell a bear exactly like one pictured in this section but if yours has worn, soiled, or damaged fur, your asking price should be lowered accordingly. The same rule applies to disfigured heads, loose limbs, destroyed paws, broken mechanisms, and any other damages the bear may have incurred. Keep this in mind if you are buying a bear as well. If it is overpriced and very damaged, look for a better buy.

The height in inches listed with each bear, if not exact, is a close approximation. Bears of the same design may not always measure the same length, due to differences in the amount of stuffing in each.

One word about eyes, too. As we have stated previously, many were removed for safety reasons during the owner's childhood. Replacements, if they are genuinely old, should not detract from a bear's value. Acceptable replacements are old shoe buttons (the flat-back type fit the head better than the rounded-back) and glass stickpin eyes.

Genuinely old handmade clothes, obviously custom-sewn for the bear wearing them, also are a value plus to many buyers. A bear with its own period wardrobe would command a higher price, even if those clothes were made after the bear was purchased.

Meanwhile, lots of good luck and happy bear hunting!

Large Mechanical Bear

25 inches; fur over papier mâché body; carved head; glass eyes; mechanism makes head move up and down.
$950

Little Dressed Cub

Royal Cub

Piano Player

Teddy Bears

Little Dressed Cub
2½ inches;
1970s; Shackman;
plush; jointed limbs;
swivel head.
$5

Royal Cub
3 inches;
Schuco; plush over
metal; black
button-type eyes;
black sewn nose and
mouth; jointed limbs;
swivel head; pin on
back so bear can be
worn as jewelry;
metal crown on head;
some have banners
across chest reading
"Berliner."
$85 and up

Piano Player
3½ inches;
circa 1950s; Steiff;
gold mohair; black
button-type eyes;
black sewn nose and
mouth; jointed limbs;
swivel head.
$150
Handmade wood
piano, elaborate: $50

Bear Trio

Nutshell Bear

Bear Trio
3 ½ inches to 5 ½ inches;
early 1900s; Steiff; white mohair; shoe button eyes; jointed limbs; swivel heads; humps.
$150 and up each

Nutshell Bear
3 ½ inches;
German; Schuco; tan mohair; black sewn nose and mouth; jointed limbs; swivel head.
Molded Nutshell: German; paper; added later.
Nutshell: $10
Bear: $75 and up

Baby Bear
3 ½ inches;
early 1900s; Steiff; mohair; straw stuffed; shoe button eyes; black sewn nose and mouth; jointed limbs; swivel head.
$150 and up

Baby Bear

Long-nose Bear

Two-faced Bear, both faces

Bear Pals

Long-nose Bear
3½ inches;
1950s; German;
brown mohair; paper
and cotton stuffed;
brown sewn nose and
mouth; jointed limbs.
$15

Two-faced Bear
3½ inches;
circa 1950; German;
Schuco; brown plush;
black button-type
eyes; black sewn nose
and mouth; jointed
limbs; screw at
bottom turns head to
reveal second face.
$150 and up

Bear Pals
3½ inches and
5½ inches;
Steiff; gold mohair;
straw stuffed; black
sewn noses and
mouths; jointed
limbs; swivel heads.
3½ inches: $125
5½ inches: $150 and
up

Panda Pals

Gymnast Bear, two positions

Little "Yes-No" Bear

Dancing Bear

Panda Pals
(left) 3½ inches; Steiff; mohair; black shoe button type eyes; flexible limbs; swivel head.
(right) 3½ inches; Schuco; mohair over metal; shoe button type eyes; jointed limbs; swivel head.
Steiff: $35 and up
Schuco: $85 and up

Gymnast Bear
4 inches; Schuco; mohair; blue felt trousers; red felt vest; wind-up mechanism makes him somersault.
$175

Little "Yes-No" Bear
4¾ inches; 1950s; German; beige mohair; black sewn nose and mouth; jointed limbs. Tail moves head up and down and from side to side.
$200

Dancing Bear
5 inches; Schuco; mohair over metal; original red bellhop outfit; black metal eyes; black sewn nose and mouth; wind-up mechanism makes bear dance and spin.
$150

Animal Trainer

Circus Bear

Simple Bear

Animal Trainer

5½ inches; circa 1910; Steiff; gold mohair; shoe button eyes; black sewn nose and mouth; jointed limbs; swivel head; hump. Pull-toy Donkey: gray felt; shoe button eyes; old metal bell; red felt saddle; leather harness; wood wheels; head bobs up and down as it rolls. Donkey: $100 Bear: $150 and up

Circus Bear

5½ inches; gold mohair over papier mâché; original leather muzzle and chain; wind-up mechanism makes head move from side to side; right leg raises and waves. $200

Simple Bear

5½ inches; circa 1920s; brown mohair; original red glass eyes; jointed limbs; swivel head. $85

Bedtime Bears

Pouting Bear

Steiff's "Jackie"

Bedtime Bears
6 inches;
early 1900s; Steiff;
brown mohair; straw
stuffed; glass eyes;
brown sewn noses
and mouths; jointed
limbs; swivel heads;
original ribbons.
Wooden Bed: maple.
Bed: $15
Bears: $150 each

Pouting Bear
6 inches;
1950s;
Knickerbocker;
brown plush; foam
stuffed; molded face;
not jointed, in
permanent sitting
position.
$10

Steiff's "Jackie"
6½ inches;
1953; mohair; brown
sewn nose (with
single white stitch)
and mouth; felt paws;
jointed limbs; swivel
head; squeaker;
elongated muzzle;
original red ribbon
around neck; "Jubilee
Teddy" on original
tag; "U.S. zone–
Germany" on label
under right arm.
Jackie was the
50-year Steiff
commemorative bear
(1903–1953).
$300 and up

Berg Bear

Bear-at-Brunch

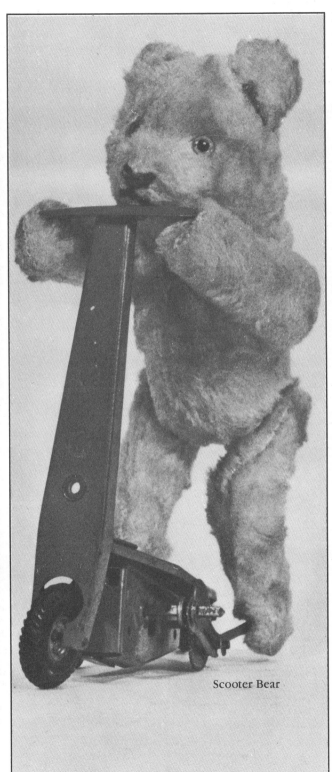

Scooter Bear

Berg Bear
6½ inches;
Berg, made in
Austria; gold plush;
straw stuffed; glass
eyes; jointed limbs;
swivel head; original
clothes.
Berg Mouse: wears
original Berg heart,
usually found on this
company's toys.
Bear: $85
Mouse: $35

Bear-at-Brunch
7 inches;
early 1900s; German;
gold mohair; straw
stuffed; glass stickpin
eyes; black sewn nose
and mouth; jointed
limbs; swivel head,
long muzzle.
$150
Akro Agate cup: $5

Scooter Bear
7 inches (including
wheels);
plush; "U.S. zone–
Germany" on metal
scooter; wind-up
mechanism.
In working condition:
$150

Little-bodied Bear

Wind-up Walker

Little-bodied Bear

8 inches; early 1900s; mohair; glass eyes; brown, sewn, elongated muzzle; felt paws; jointed limbs; swivel head; squeaker; hump; very appealing.
$150 and up

Wind-up Walker

8 inches; 1920s; German; Gebrüder-Bing; mohair; shoe button eyes; black sewn nose and mouth; felt paws; wooden walking stick; original yellow felt jacket and blue cotton pants.
$400 and up

Schuco's "Rolly"

8½ inches; German; brown mohair; roller skating wind-up; "Made in U.S. Zone–Germany" on tag.
$300

Schuco's "Rolly"

Traveling Trio

Circus Clown Bear

Big Bow Bear

Traveling Trio
8½ inches;
early 1900s; German;
brown mohair; straw
stuffed; shoe button
eyes; black sewn
noses and mouths;
felt paws; jointed
limbs; swivel heads;
humps.
$650 for the trio
Fitted travel trunk:
$25

Circus Clown Bear
9 inches;
early 1900s; Steiff;
gold mohair; straw
stuffed; glass eyes;
black sewn nose and
mouth; felt paws;
jointed limbs; swivel
head; hump; original
clown hat and ruffled
collar.
$400

Big Bow Bear
9 inches;
1907; Steiff; gold
mohair; straw
stuffed; shoe button
eyes; black sewn nose
and mouth; felt paws;
jointed limbs; swivel
head; squeaker;
hump; finest quality.
$350

Tumbling Bear, two positions

Baby Wool Bear

Cocoa Bear

Tumbling Bear
9½ inches;
1920s; German;
Gebrüder-Bing;
original green felt
jacket and yellow
pants; wind-up arms
enable bear to
somersault; "BW" on
metal arm tag.
$400

Baby Wool Bear
9½ inches;
early 1900s; brown
wool; straw stuffed;
shoe button eyes;
black sewn nose and
mouth; felt paws;
jointed limbs; swivel
head.
$175

Cocoa Bear
10 inches;
1940s; Character;
brown plush; soft
stuffed; black
button-type eyes
fastened over white
felt.
$25

Old Friends

Old Friends

10 inches; (left)
early 1900s; German; brown wool; straw stuffed; shoe button eyes; black sewn nose and mouth; swivel head; metal wheels.
13 inches; (right)
early 1900s; gold mohair; straw stuffed; glass stickpin eyes; black sewn nose and mouth; felt paws; wide-set ears; jointed limbs; swivel head; fat body; hump.
Wheeled bear: $300 and up
Standing bear: $300

Sunday Driver Bears

Sunday Driver Bears

10 inches and 8 inches;
1960s; German; gold mohair; glass-type eyes; felt paws; jointed limbs; swivel heads; squeakers.
8 inches: $85
10 inches: $100

Perky Panda

Pulling Bear

Perky Panda
11 inches;
Steiff; mohair; open
mouth; gray felt
paws; squeaker;
jointed limbs; swivel
head; hard to find.
$250

Pulling Bear
10½ inches;
Steiff "Teddy Baby";
brown mohair;
slightly cross-eyed;
open mouth; felt
paws; jointed limbs;
swivel head; very
cute.
$150 and up

Riding Bear

Riding Bear
11 inches;
plush; soft stuffed;
blue and white
checked body; metal
tricycle with red
wooden wheels; legs
pedal as trike is
pulled.
$125

Roller Skater

Bellhop Bear

Roller Skater
11 inches;
1930s; long-haired
mohair; soft stuffed;
glass stickpin eyes;
black sewn nose and
mouth; jointed limbs
(clothes and skates
not original).
$110

Bellhop Bear
11 inches;
mohair; straw
stuffed; shoe button
eyes; black sewn nose
and mouth; felt paws;
jointed limbs; swivel
head; red felt jacket
and hat; very large
feet; tail movement
controls head; rare.
$400 and up

Playmate Bear

Playmate Bear
11 inches;
1950s; English:
Twyford; gold
mohair; soft stuffed;
black sewn nose and
mouth; cloth paws;
jointed limbs; swivel
head.
$65
Roddy plastic
walking doll; 1950s;
England.
$65

Pink Bear

Tough-guy Bear

Bird-watching Bear

Pink Bear
11½ inches;
circa 1920s; rare pink
mohair; soft stuffed;
glass eyes; black sewn
nose and mouth;
fabric paws; jointed
limbs; swivel head.
$200

Tough-guy Bear
12 inches;
1930s; gold mohair;
straw stuffed; glass
eyes; black sewn nose
and mouth; felt paws;
jointed limbs; swivel
head; pouty face.
$200

**Bird-watching
Bear**
12 inches;
dark brown mohair;
straw stuffed; black
sewn nose and
mouth; felt paws;
short, stocky body;
chubby jointed limbs;
swivel head.
$150
Marx wind-up parrot;
blinking eyes;
flapping wings;
chirps.
$65

Country Cub

Hockey Player

Perky Bear

Laughing Bear

Country Cub
12 inches;
1950s; German; tail
(yes-no) mechanism;
mohair head and
paws; cloth body;
glass eyes; black sewn
nose and mouth;
jointed limbs;
original clothes.
$400 and up
Gund Donald Duck;
1950s.
$65

Hockey Player
12 inches;
1970s; Steiff; soft
stuffed; open felt
mouth; original
hockey stick and very
realistic skates; hard
to find.
$175 and up

Perky Bear
12 inches;
early 1900s; Ideal;
mohair; straw and
excelsior stuffed;
shoe button eyes;
black sewn nose and
mouth; large felt
paws; jointed limbs;
swivel head;
distinctive face and
expression; very rare.
$300 and up

Laughing Bear
12 inches;
shaggy brown
mohair; straw
stuffed; glass eyes;
black sewn nose;
open felt mouth; felt
paws; jointed limbs;
swivel head.
$150

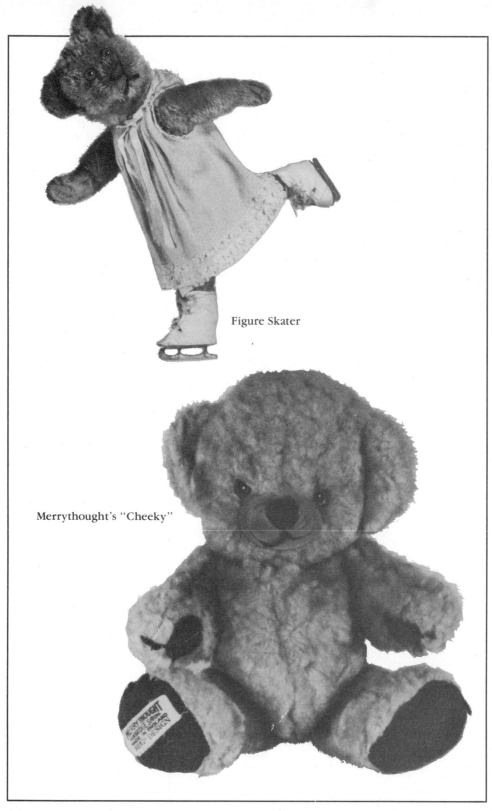

Figure Skater

Merrythought's "Cheeky"

Hi, There Bear

Figure Skater
12 inches;
early 1900s; gold
mohair; straw
stuffed; glass stickpin
eyes; black sewn nose
and mouth; felt paws;
jointed limbs; swivel
head; squeaker;
hump.
$175

Merrythought's "Cheeky"
12 inches;
English; light brown
plush; jointed limbs;
swivel head; unusual
face; label on right
foot; very well made.
$70

Hi, There Bear
12 inches;
Steiff; gold mohair;
straw stuffed; glass
eyes; brown sewn
nose and mouth; felt
paws; jointed limbs;
swivel head; squeaker
(stand not original).
$150

Dressed Country Bears

Dressed Country Bears

12 inches; modern; Steiff; soft stuffed; original clothes; sold exclusively by F.A.O. Schwarz, New York. Each: $150 and up

Bon Vivants

12 inches; early 1900s; Steiff; mohair; straw stuffed; shoe button eyes; black sewn noses and mouths; felt paws; jointed limbs; swivel heads; squeakers; humps. Each $250 and up

Bon Vivants

Casual Bear

Quizzical Bear

Worn-patch Bear

Casual Bear
13 inches;
early 1900s; Steiff;
mohair; straw
stuffed; shoe button
eyes; felt paws;
jointed limbs; swivel
head; hump.
$300 and up

Quizzical Bear
13 inches;
early 1900s; soft
brown mohair; straw
stuffed; glass eyes;
elongated muzzle
with black sewn
nose, and mouth; felt
paws; wide-set ears;
jointed limbs; swivel
head; squeaker;
hump; very nice,
unusual expression.
$300 and up

Worn-patch Bear
13 inches;
early 1900s; Steiff;
gold mohair; straw
stuffed; shoe button
eyes; black sewn nose
and mouth; felt paws;
jointed limbs; swivel
head; growler; hump;
worn spots on body.
$185

Ice Skaters

Short-hair Bear

Serious Bear

Ice Skaters
13 inches; early 1900s; gold mohair; straw stuffed; glass stickpin eyes; black sewn noses and mouths; felt paws; jointed limbs; swivel heads; squeakers; skates and clothes not original. $175 each

Short-hair Bear
13 inches; gold plush; soft stuffed; black button eyes; black sewn nose and mouth; velvet paws; jointed limbs; round, swivel head; elongated muzzle. $75

Serious Bear
13 inches; circa 1920s; brown mohair; straw stuffed; glass eyes; brown sewn nose and mouth; felt paws; jointed limbs; swivel head; squeaker; small hump; very appealing. $200

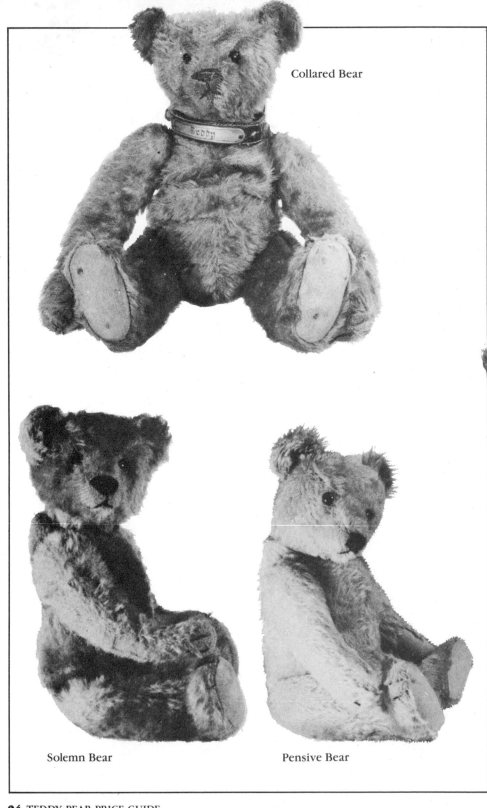

Collared Bear

Solemn Bear

Pensive Bear

Attentive Bear

Collared Bear
13 inches;
early 1900s; Steiff;
brown mohair; straw
stuffed; jointed limbs;
old collar with
engraved "Teddy"
tag, not original.
$300 and up

Solemn Bear
13 inches;
early 1900s; Steiff;
gold mohair; straw
stuffed; shoe button
eyes; black sewn nose
and mouth; felt paws;
jointed limbs; swivel
head; squeaker;
hump.
$250 and up

Pensive Bear
13 inches;
1920s; light brown
mohair; straw
stuffed; glass eyes;
black sewn nose and
mouth; felt paws;
jointed limbs; swivel
head; squeaker; small
hump.
$200

Attentive Bear
13 inches;
Steiff; straw stuffed;
glass eyes; black sewn
nose and mouth; felt
paws; jointed limbs;
swivel head; hump.
$200

Baggy Bear

Tyrolean Teddy

Over-stuffed Bear

Baggy Bear
13 inches;
1950s; light green
plush head and paws;
baggy body of cotton
chintz; soft stuffed;
black plastic nose.
Krueger Pig:
7½ inches;
cloth molded head;
cloth body.
Bear: $15
Pig: $25

Tyrolean Teddy
13 inches;
tan mohair; straw
stuffed; glass type
eyes; black sewn nose
and mouth; felt paws;
flat standing feet;
tail-moves-head
mechanism; original
clothes; unusually
appealing.
$500 and up

Over-stuffed Bear
13 inches;
1940s; dark brown
mohair; soft stuffed;
glass stickpin eyes;
felt muzzle with black
sewn nose and
mouth; felt upper
paws; cuddly
appearance.
$75

Bat-eared Bear

Herr Bear

Bat-eared Bear
13 inches;
early 1900s; gold
mohair; sawdust
stuffed; shoe button
eyes; black sewn nose
and mouth; felt paws;
jointed limbs; swivel
head.
$250

Herr Bear
13½ inches;
circa 1920; German;
gold mohair; glass
stickpin eyes; black
sewn nose and
mouth; felt paws;
wide-set ears; jointed
limbs; swivel head;
unusual facial
expression.
$250 and up

Twin "Peter" Teddies

Farmer Bear

Twin "Peter" Teddies

14 inches;
1920s; German;
Gebrüder Süssenguth;
mohair (brown grizzle
or gray grizzle); wood
or glass eyes; realistic
teeth; movable bisque
tongues; jointed
limbs; swivel heads.
Considered very rare.
Tin basin set: $225
Bears: $900 and up
each

Farmer Bear

13½ inches;
gold mohair; straw
stuffed; glass eyes;
black sewn nose and
mouth; felt paws;
jointed limbs; swivel
head; squeaker; very
hard to the touch.
$175

Dynamic Duo

14 inches;
early 1900s; German;
dark gold mohair;
straw stuffed; shoe
button eyes; black
sewn noses and
mouths; felt paws;
jointed limbs; swivel
heads; humps; very
elongated muzzles.
$650 and up for
matched pair

Dynamic Duo

"Feedme"

Funny-faced Bear

Very Sweet Bear

"Feedme"
14 inches;
1930s;
Commonwealth Toy & Novelty Company; brown mohair; soft stuffed; glass eyes; black sewn nose; head tips back to reveal internal metal mouth, throat, and tummy. Bear was made to "eat" crackers, which then could be removed through zipper in back.
Bear with original advertising poster: $250

Funny-faced Bear
14 inches;
1920s; gold mohair; straw stuffed; glass stickpin eyes; black sewn nose and mouth; felt paws; jointed limbs; swivel head.
Little Cottage: old wooden string holder with lift-off top.
Cottage: $35
Bear: $200

Very Sweet Bear
14 inches;
1920s; gold mohair; straw stuffed; glass stickpin eyes; black sewn nose and mouth; felt paws; jointed limbs; swivel head.
$175

Rare Bear Pair

Rare Bear Pair
15 inches;
early 1900s; Steiff;
white mohair; soft
stuffed; shoe button
eyes; light brown
sewn noses and
mouths; felt paws;
jointed limbs; swivel
heads; squeakers;
humps; rare pair;
more valuable as a
matched set.
$400 and up each

Steiff's "Cosy Teddy"
15 inches;
1970s; white plush
with brown under
neck; soft stuffed;
glass-like eyes; brown
sewn nose; open felt
mouth; felt paws.
$150 and up

Steiff's "Cosy Teddy"

Steiff's "Minky Zotty"

Surprised Bear

Small-eared Bear

Steiff's "Minky Zotty"
15 inches;
1970s;
platinum-mink-colored plush; brown sewn nose; felt open mouth; growler; luxurious texture and appearance.
Tin Box: squeaking wooden clown pops out when button at bottom is pulled.
Box: $60
Bear: $150 and up

Surprised Bear
15 inches;
1930s; brown mohair; soft stuffed; glass stickpin eyes; black sewn nose and mouth; felt paws; jointd limbs; swivel head.
Old Wind-up Birds: German; plush-covered metal bodies.
Bird Pair: $40
Bear: $140

Small-eared Bear
15 inches;
early 1900s; white mohair, straw stuffed; glass stickpin eyes light brown sewn nose and mouth; linen paws; jointed limbs; swivel head; thin limbs.
$200

Yellow Fellow

Good Listener

Orange Bear

Yellow Fellow
15 inches;
Character; yellow-gold
mohair; soft stuffed;
black button type
eyes; black sewn nose
and mouth; jointed
limbs; swivel head;
round face and
muzzle; plump torso
and limbs.
$75

Good Listener
15 inches;
beige mohair; straw
stuffed; shoe button
eyes; black sewn nose
and mouth; jointed
limbs; swivel head;
very wide-set ears.
$150

Orange Bear
15 inches;
1940s; orange
mohair; straw
stuffed; glass stickpin
eyes; black sewn nose
and mouth; pink felt
paws; jointed limbs;
swivel head;
squeaker.
$125

Music Maker

Irresistible Bear

Sweet-looking Bear

Music Maker
15 inches;
circa 1930s; long
white mohair; glass
eyes; black sewn nose
and mouth; felt paws;
jointed limbs; swivel
head; music box in
torso activated by
squeezing; unusual.
$400 and up

Irresistible Bear
15 inches;
1910–1920; straw
stuffed; shoe button
eyes; black sewn nose
and mouth; felt paws;
jointed limbs; swivel
head; squeaker;
hump.
$400 and up

Sweet-looking
Bear
15 inches;
early 1900s; gold
mohair; straw and
kapok stuffed; shoe
button eyes; black
sewn nose and
mouth; hard-soled
feet; very wide-set
ears; jointed limbs;
swivel head;
squeaker; hump.
$400 and up

Dancing Bear Pair

Staring Bear

Englishbear

Dancing Bear Pair
15 inches and
12 inches;
circa 1910; Steiff;
glass eyes; sewn
noses and mouths;
jointed limbs; swivel
heads; male bear
dressed in blue jacket
and blue plaid pants;
female bear's dress
has blue skirt and
violet bodice (original
clothes); bears are
attached at paws and
shoulders; rare.
$1,400 and up

Staring Bear
15 inches;
1930s; gold mohair;
straw stuffed; glass
stickpin eyes; black
sewn nose and
mouth; jointed limbs;
swivel head; hump;
thin torso and limbs.
$200

Englishbear
15 inches;
1950s; English; Chad
Valley; gold mohair;
soft stuffed; black
sewn nose and
mouth; brown felt
paws; jointed limbs;
swivel head.
$75 and up

Ideal's Collector's Edition

"Gentle Ben"

Studious Bear

Jerome

Ideal's Collector's Edition
16 inches;
1978; 75th anniversary commemorative; brown plush; lighter muzzle and paws; "The Original Ideal Teddy Bear" on tag; special edition box.
$50

"Gentle Ben"
16 inches;
1967; Mattel (Ivan Tors Films, Inc. character); black plush; plastic eyes; pink open mouth with red felt tongue; black plastic nose; pull-string voice box.
$35 and up

Studious Bear
16 inches;
circa 1930s; long, wavy yellow-gold mohair; straw stuffed; glass eyes; black sewn nose and mouth; felt paws; jointed limbs; swivel head.
Walt Disney book: 1930s.
Bear: $140

Jerome
16 inches;
early 1900s; mohair; soft stuffed; shoe button eyes; wearing vintage clothing; named by current owner; rare.
$350 and up

Charismatic Cub

Bird-Brain

Charismatic Cub
16 inches;
early 1900s; Steiff;
blank button; brown
mohair; straw
stuffed; shoe button
eyes; black sewn nose
and mouth; felt paws;
jointed limbs; swivel
head; chubby; rare.
$600 and up

Bird-Brain
16 inches;
white mohair; straw
stuffed; glass stickpin
eyes; black sewn nose
and mouth; felt paws;
jointed limbs; swivel
head.
Steiff Parrot:
5 inches; mohair.
Bear: $150
Parrot: $65

Jester Bear

100th Anniversary Bear

Steiff's "Zotty"

Jester Bear

16 inches; early 1900s; German; green mohair body; straw stuffed; shoe button eyes; elongated nose; swivel head; very long arms; original felt clown collar and cuffs.
$350 and up

100th Anniversary Bear

17 inches; Steiff commemorative (1880–1980); limited edition of 11,000; numbered ear tag; reproduction of the 1903 original; mohair; jointed limbs; swivel head; includes special box and official signed certificate.
$375 and up

Steiff's "Zotty"

17 inches; brown-and-cream shaded fur; brown sewn nose; open felt mouth; felt paws; jointed limbs; swivel head; growler.
$150 and up

Bulky Bear

Bulky Bear
17 inches;
early 1900s; cotton
fabric; straw stuffed;
shoe button eyes;
original clothes;
unusual.
$300

Santa Bear
17 inches;
white mohair; soft
stuffed; glass stickpin
eyes; jointed arms;
floppy legs; swivel
head; wind-up music
box plays "Jingle
Bells"; replaced Santa
Claus suit.
$125

Smiling Bear
17 inches;
1950s; Ideal; brown
plush; soft stuffed;
plastic eyes; molded
nose and mouth;
cream plush paws;
squeaker in tail.
$50

Santa Bear

Smiling Bear

Playtime Bear

Flower Bear

Playtime Bear
17 inches;
brown mohair; soft
stuffed, some
excelsior; shoe
button eyes; black
sewn nose and
mouth; cloth
replacement paws;
hump.
Fisher-Price musical
wood Teddy Bear
pull-toy.
Bear: $300
Pull-toy: $25

Flower Bear
17 inches;
1920s; gold mohair;
straw stuffed; glass
stickpin eyes; black
sewn nose and
mouth; replaced felt
paws; jointed limbs;
swivel head.
$175 and up

Mighty Mouth

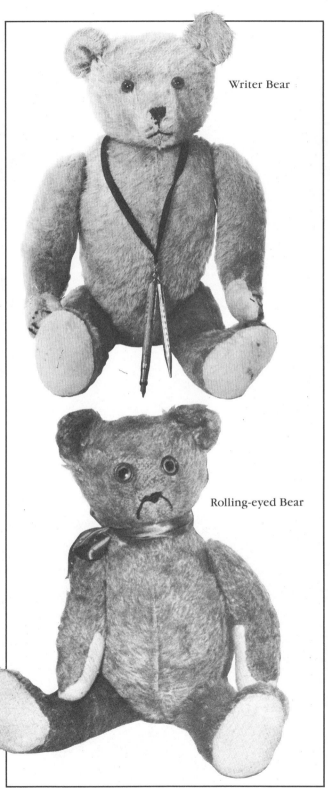

Writer Bear

Rolling-eyed Bear

Mighty Mouth

17 inches;
brown mohair; soft
stuffed; glass type
eyes; black sewn nose
and mouth; also red
felt open mouth
which opens and
closes by means of
rod mechanism in
back of head; jointed
limbs; swivel head.
$200 and up

Writer Bear

18 inches;
1920s; gold mohair;
straw stuffed; glass
stickpin eyes; black
sewn nose and
mouth; felt paws;
jointed limbs; swivel
head.
(Gold 1920s fountain
pen and pencil are
added.)
Bear: $175 and up

Rolling-eyed Bear

18 inches;
1920s; gold mohair;
straw stuffed (some
of these bears were
stuffed with cork);
rolling eyes in metal
rims; felt paws;
jointed limbs; swivel
head.
$400 and up

Friendly Bear

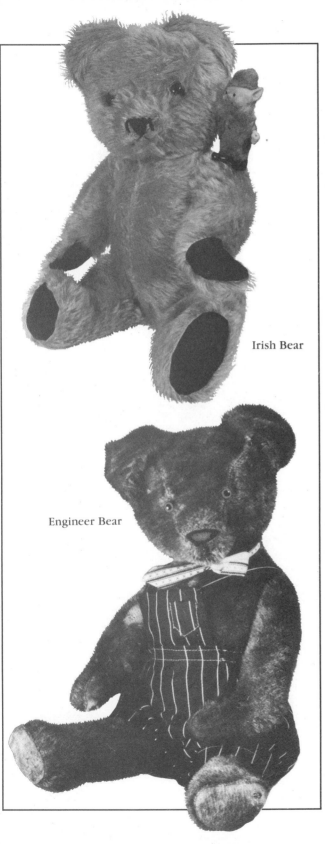

Irish Bear

Engineer Bear

Friendly Bear
19 inches;
circa 1940s; white
mohair; soft stuffed;
glass stickpin eyes;
black sewn nose and
mouth; felt paws;
jointed limbs; swivel
head; squeaker.
Old White Mohair
Dog: Steiff; straw
stuffed; stickpin eyes;
swivel head;
squeaker.
Dog: $125
Bear: $200 and up

Irish Bear
19 inches;
1940s; yellow-gold
mohair; safety
(secured) eyes; black
sewn nose and
mouth; fabric paws;
jointed limbs; swivel
head; chubby body;
"Made in Republic of
Ireland" on tag.
Leprechaun is from
the 1970s and added
for good luck.
Leprechaun: $2
Bear: $110

Engineer Bear
19 inches;
brown mohair; glass
eyes; jointed limbs;
swivel head.
$200 and up

Grizzly Bear

Heart-faced Bear

Alert Bear

Grizzly Bear
19 inches;
early 1900s; fluffy
gold mohair; straw
stuffed; glass stickpin
eyes; brown sewn
nose and mouth; felt
paws; jointed limbs;
swivel head; hump;
realistic appearance;
rare.
$400 and up

Heart-faced Bear
19 inches;
circa 1920s; gold
mohair; straw
stuffed; shoe button
eyes; black sewn nose
and mouth; felt paws;
jointed limbs; swivel
head; squeaker; hump
unusual expression.
$200

Alert Bear
19 inches;
1920s; gold mohair;
straw stuffed; glass
eyes; black sewn nose
and mouth; original
felt paws replaced;
jointed limbs; swivel
head; stiff, elongated
torso.
$125

Clown Bear

Teddy Bear Doll

Clown Bear
19 inches;
early 1900s; gold
mohair; straw
stuffed; glass stickpin
eyes; black sewn nose
and mouth; felt paws;
wide-set ears; jointed
limbs; swivel head;
original clown suit
replaced.
$165

Teddy Bear Doll
19 inches;
cloth-covered,
sack-type torso and
limbs; mohair head;
straw and cork
stuffed; glass eyes;
black sewn thin nose
and mouth; felt paws;
swivel head; original
black and yellow suit.
$200

Inquisitive Bear

Ursa Major

Inquisitive Bear
19 inches;
1920s; gold mohair;
straw stuffed; glass
stickpin eyes; black
sewn nose and
mouth; jointed limbs;
swivel head.
$125

Ursa Major
20 inches;
early 1900s; German;
gold mohair; straw
stuffed; shoe button
eyes; black sewn nose
and mouth; large felt
paws; long jointed
limbs; swivel head;
hump; unusually fine
quality.
Dresser circa 1900:
$175
Bear: $500 and up

Autographed Bear
20 inches;
1970s; English; Peggy
Nisbet; mohair; soft
stuffed; black sewn
nose and mouth;
jointed limbs; swivel
head; "Autographed
Collector's Edition"
on tag.
$100 and up

Autographed Bear

Sociable Bear

Sociable Bear
20 inches;
1920s; gold mohair;
straw stuffed; glass
stickpin eyes; felt
paws; jointed limbs;
swivel head.
Willow Pattern Doll
Tea Set: service for
four, plus pot,
creamer and sugar
bowl in original box.
Tea Set: $75 and up
Bear: $175

Literary Bear
20 inches;
early 1900s; brown
mohair; straw
stuffed; glass eyes;
black sewn nose and
mouth; felt paws;
jointed limbs; swivel
head; exceptional
quality.
Book: *Der faule
Teddybär;* inscription
dated 1928; German;
color plates.
Book: $100
Bear: $500 and up

Literary Bear

Very Important Bear

Shaggy Chap

Very Important Bear
20 inches;
early 1900s; Steiff;
silky, light gold
mohair; straw
stuffed; large shoe
button eyes; brown
sewn nose and
mouth; felt paws;
jointed limbs; swivel
head; hump; long
arms; large feet;
extremely appealing;
rare in this size and
condition.
$400 and up

Shaggy Chap
20 inches;
1930s; reddish brown
mohair; soft stuffed;
glass eyes; black sewn
nose and mouth; felt
paws; jointed limbs;
swivel head; hump.
$300

Crossed-paws Bear
20 inches;
1938; Knickerbocker;
brown mohair; soft
stuffed; glass eyes;
black sewn nose and
mouth; velvet paws;
jointed limbs; swivel
head; round face.
$300

Crossed-paws Bear

Turned-up Nose Bear

Thoughtful Bear

Open-mouth Bear

Nosy Bear

Turned-up Nose Bear
21 inches; early 1900s; gold mohair; straw stuffed; glass stickpin eyes; black sewn nose and mouth; felt paws; jointed limbs; swivel head; hump; old brass chain around neck. $250

Thoughtful Bear
21 inches; 1930s; gold mohair; straw stuffed; glass stickpin eyes; brown sewn nose and mouth; felt paws; jointed limbs; swivel head; pear-shaped torso. $300

Open-mouth Bear
21 inches; 1939–40; Knickerbocker; brown mohair; soft stuffed; glass stickpin eyes; brown sewn nose; felt mouth; felt paws; jointed limbs; swivel head; growler in body. $300

Nosy Bear
21 inches; circa 1930s; cinnamon mohair; soft stuffed; black glass stickpin eyes; black sewn nose and mouth; velvet paws; jointed limbs; swivel head; squeaker; modified hump. $150 and up

Super Bear

Cinnamon Bear

Super Bear

21 inches;
Steiff; gold mohair;
straw stuffed; glass
eyes; black sewn nose
and mouth; felt paws;
jointed limbs; swivel
head; growler; hump;
finest quality.
$400

Cinnamon Bear

21 inches;
cinnamon mohair;
straw stuffed; shoe
button eyes; brown
sewn nose and
mouth; felt paws;
jointed limbs; large
swivel head;
squeaker; hump;
plump torso and
limbs.
$300

Concertmaster

Concertmaster

21 inches;
light gold mohair;
straw stuffed; glass
stickpin eyes; black
sewn nose and
mouth; felt paws;
thin jointed limbs;
swivel head; hump.
Tin violin; original
bow; 1930s.
Violin: $25
Bear: $300

Teatime Teddy

Teatime Teddy

21 inches;
German; gold mohair;
straw stuffed; glass
eyes; black sewn nose
and mouth; felt paws;
hard-soled feet;
jointed limbs; tail
moves head up and
down, side to side.
All bears of this type
are coined "Yes-No"
bears and are highly
sought after.
Blue Willow Tea Set:
$75 and up
Bear: $600 and up

"Roddy"

22 inches;
English; mohair; glass
eyes; black sewn nose
and mouth; felt paws;
jointed limbs; tail
moves head up and
down, or from side to
side; very unusual;
"Roddy" on tag.
$700 and up

"Roddy"

Baggy Bear

Black Bear, Esq.

Baggy Bear
23 inches;
early 1900s; mohair;
glass stickpin eyes;
jointed limbs; swivel
head; hump;
heart-shaped face.
$375 and up

Black Bear, Esq.
23 inches;
rich black mohair;
straw stuffed; glass
stickpin eyes; light
brown sewn nose and
mouth; tan paws;
jointed limbs; swivel
head; hump; a
wonderful,
hard-to-find bear.
$375 and up

Sailor Bear

Electric-eye Bear

Large Bear

Battery Bear

Electric-eye Bear

23 inches;
1918–19; red, white,
and blue mohair;
straw stuffed; glass
bulb eyes; black sewn
nose and mouth;
jointed at shoulders;
press stomach to
activate battery in
torso which lights up
eyes; unusual.
In working condition:
$300 and up

Sailor Bear

23 inches;
1920s; German; short
gold mohair; straw
stuffed; glass stickpin
eyes; black sewn nose
and mouth; felt paws;
very loosely jointed;
swivel head.
$175

Large Bear

24 inches;
English; gold mohair;
straw stuffed; glass
stickpin eyes; black
sewn nose and
mouth; replaced felt
paws; jointed limbs;
swivel head; very
chubby torso.
$250 and up

Battery Bear

24 inches;
1918–19; white
mohair; straw
stuffed; jointed arms;
battery pack in back
gives power to light-
bulb eyes.
In working condition:
$300 and up

Louisa

Louisa
26 inches;
English; gray mohair;
straw stuffed; glass
stickpin eyes; black
fabric nose, sewn
mouth; replaced felt
paws; named by
current owner.
Silverlocks: $15
Bear: $350 and up

George's Bear

George's Bear
27 inches;
1936; brown mohair;
soft stuffed; glass
eyes; black sewn nose
and mouth; velvet
paws; jointed limbs;
swivel head; named
for original owner.
$275

Big Foot

Big Foot
36 inches;
Steiff; light gold
mohair; glass eyes;
brown sewn nose;
felt open mouth and
paws; jointed limbs;
swivel head; growler
mechanism operated
by wire pulled from
back; hump; "U.S.
Zone–Germany" on
tag.
$1,500

Teddy Threesome

Four-wheeler

German Nodder

Bears on All Fours

Teddy Threesome
5 inches high;
Steiff; mohair; swivel
heads; stationary legs;
leather-like collars
with bells; felt paws.
$65 each

Four-wheeler
8 inches high;
(including wheels);
Steiff; mohair; glass
eyes; swivel head;
squeaker; metal
wheels; tail.
$300

German Nodder
10 inches high;
German; turn of the
century; mohair over
papier mâché; glass
stickpin eyes;
wind-up mechansim
makes head nod and
bear growl; original
leather muzzle; very
rare.
$1,000

Steiff's "Fellow"

Old Growler

Steiff's "Fellow"

11 inches high (including wheels); dark brown mohair; straw stuffed; glass eyes; felt paws; hump; metal wheels; "Fellow" on tag.
$375

Old Growler

15 inches (including wheels); German; brown mohair; straw stuffed; glass stickpin eyes; felt paws; wood wheels; pull-ring-activated growler. In working condition: $400 and up

Rock and Roll Bear

22 inches (including wheels and rocker); turn of the century; brown mohair; shoe button eyes; black sewn nose and mouth; swivel head; original Steiff blanket and leather handled saddle; original removable wood rockers.
$800 and up

Rock and Roll Bear

Old Winnie-the-Pooh

Winnie-the-Pooh

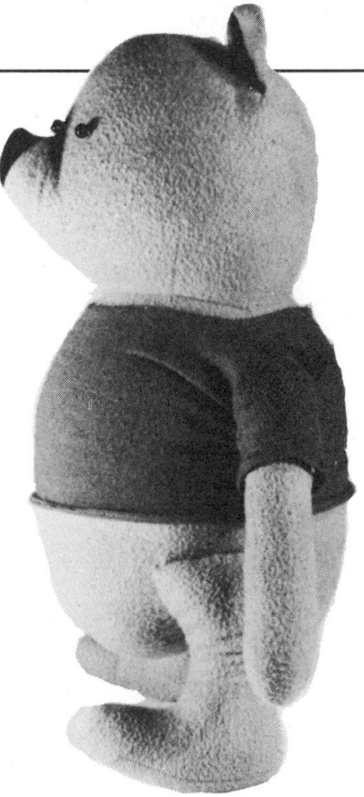

Another Winnie-the-Pooh

Fair-Bear

Not Quite Teddy Bears

Old Winnie-the-Pooh
6½ inches;
circa 1930s; English;
brown felt; glass eyes;
delicately sewn nose
and mouth; jointed
limbs.
Piglet: 4 inches; circa
1930s; pink felt; glass
eyes; delicately sewn
nose and mouth;
jointed limbs.
Pair: $150

Winnie-the-Pooh
11 inches;
English; soft stuffed;
floppy arms; red sock
hat.
$55

Another Winnie-the-Pooh
13 inches;
1950s–60s; felt; soft
stuffed; black button
eyes; black felt nose;
stitched-on limbs;
with original red
shirt.
$65

Fair-Bear
13 inches;
1982; Ace Novelty;
tan and white plush;
not jointed; ribbon
and tag read "The
1982 World's Fair.
Knoxville,
Tennessee"
$35

Three Versions of Smokey the Bear

Three Versions of Smokey the Bear

In 1953, Ideal Toy Corp. was given permission to make and sell Smokey dolls; the company also printed Junior Forest Ranger cards and packed one with each doll. Some 16,000 youngsters applied to be Junior Forest Rangers, and Ideal was honored with a "Golden Smokey" award in 1967 for its contribution.
Left: 12 inches; $25.
Center: 17 inches; molded face; glass-like eyes; $50.
Right: 16 inches; $35.

Delicate Doll

Delicate Doll

13½ inches; early 1900s; German; gray mohair; excelsior stuffed; bisque head; glass sleep-eyes; called Teddy Bear Doll or Eskimo Doll.
$350

Kellogg Bears

Koala

Kellogg Bears
Three bears, largest is 12 inches; 1920s; fabric printed with red, white, blue, and brown; soft stuffed; company premium; set includes Goldilocks (not pictured).
Set of four: $200 and up

Koala
15 inches; modern; Steiff; mohair; felt nose and open mouth; jointed limbs; swivel head; squeaker; legs are bent in curved position; bendable fingers and toes; unique appearance.
$250 and up

Knickerbocker's "Yogi Bear"
16 inches; 1959; Hanna-Barbera Productions character made by Knickerbocker; brown plush; soft stuffed; molded face; yellow paws and front; green felt tie. Original "Huckleberry Hound" from same company and year. Original pair: $85

Knickerbocker's "Yogi Bear"

Casimir

Casimir

French; mechanical: walks on all fours, *then sits up on back feet and sways from side to side.* (German and Japanese versions of this bear only walk on all fours.) Unusual quality; metal nose; glass eyes; with original circus-type box.
$300

Panda

Panda

24 inches
1940s; Character; soft stuffed; red felt tongue; floppy limbs.
$65

Perfume Holder

Compact Bear, two views

Perfume Bottle Bear,
two views

Teddy Bear Items

Perfume Holder
1½ inches;
1970s; metal; Teddy
Bear's hinged back
opens to reveal solid
Max Factor perfume.
$25

Compact Bear
3¾ inches;
early 1900s; mohair;
jointed limbs; head is
removed to show
hinged body
containing mirror;
rare.
$200 and up

Perfume Bottle
Bear
3¾ inches;
early 1900s; mohair;
black button-type
eyes; black sewn nose
and mouth; jointed
limbs; head is
removed to show
glass perfume bottle;
rare.
$200 and up

Bear Muff

Bear Muff
14 inches high; light gold mohair; glass eyes; black sewn nose; muff has quilted lining; rare. $350 and up

Attentive-bear Muff
15 inches; early 1900s; gray mohair plush; thick lining; glass eyes; black sewn nose; felt paws; rare. $350 and up

Attentive-bear Muff

Bear Books
Complete set of eight 1907 books; various adventures of "The Teddy Bears"; rhymes by Robert D. Towne; illustrations by J. R. Bray. Copyright: Judge Company and the Reilly and Britton Company. Set of 8: $125 and up

Bear Books

Bears-You-Wear

Bears-You-Wear
Assorted Teddy Bear jewelry, varying in price from $4 (stickpin) to more than $400 (large, jointed charm).

Pour-a-Panda
Giant Panda, collectors' bottle; 1980; James B. Beam Distilling Company. $15

Pour-a-Panda

China Bears

China Bears

early 1900s; German; available in many styles and sizes; easily recognizable because of green and white coloring on vase or purse; price varies depending upon appeal and number of animals per piece. Each: $75 and up

Bicycling Bear Tea Set

Bavarian china; doll-size set; decorated with bicycling bears and other animals; service for three, including teapot, sugar bowl and creamer. $75

Bear-Ware

1930s; German; doll-size tableware; service for six; bears impressed into handles; original fitted black box. $85

Bicycling Bear Tea Set

Bear-Ware

Climbing Bear, two views

Climbing Bear

6½ inches;
German; mohair;
metal eyes; jointed
limbs; does tricks on
16-inch wooden
stick.
$165

Jack-in-the-Box

8 inches;
Teddy Bear with
parasol; wood handle
turns and plays music
while bear bobs up
and down; rare.
$225

Jack-in-the-Box

Paper Dolls

Paper Dolls
10½-inch Teddy
Bear;
early 1900s; E. I.
Horsman; paper; five
outfits; two hats;
original paper
envelope.
$350

Old Chocolate Service
Lithographed tin;
Teddies on tray, cups,
pot.
$125

Old Chocolate Service

New Coffee Service
1970s; German;
plastic; doll dishes
with Teddy motif.
$10

New Coffee Service

New Bears

The following section is devoted to newer bears. The ones selected to appear on these pages were chosen because of their quality, appeal, or possible future collectibility. A few were picked because they had unusual features.

The examples shown are only a part of the wide variety of wonderful modern Teddy Bears from which you may make your choices. Because prices vary from store to store throughout the country we have not included them. The importance of some of these bears is their potential value as collectibles. But, contemporary manufacturers and designers, artists and specialists are offering creations so cuddly and cheerful, that it shouldn't matter whether or not some of them become collectible—they make irresistible companions.

Kimberly Port's "Bearina and Muff"

Although a few modern bears are covered with mohair, many are made with man-made plush fabrics. Stuffing materials are also modern, since safety regulations and practices find straw and excelsior to be too flammable.

In most cases, these bears have shatterproof eyes securely fastened into their heads, since glass stickpin eyes are also considered too hazardous for young children. Some bears have features which are dyed or molded rather than embroidered.

Although these bears were available at the time of publication, if you have difficulty finding any you would like to own, consult the directory on page 212 for the manufacturer's or importer's address and telephone number. Some, however, may have been discontinued.

New Bear Guide

Bearina and Muff
1½ inches; jointed limbs; swivel head; comes with ⅝-inch muff; handmade by artist Kimberly Port. Note elaborate clothes, high-button shoes, handmade box.

Steiff Trio
5 inches; mohair; white, caramel, or beige; jointed limbs; swivel heads; 10,000 made in 1983.

Steiff Trio

Elegant Lady

Berg Bear

Elegant Lady
1½ inches;
fully jointed;
handmade by artist
Sara Phillips; elegant
outfit includes hat,
fur-trimmed hooded
cape, detailed gown.

Berg Bear
2¾ inches
(sitting);
Austrian; Berg; plush;
flexible limbs; swivel
head; heart tag.

Fuzzy Friends
2¼ inches;
fabric over sculpture;
fully jointed; some
with tail-moves-head
action; handmade by
artist April
Whitcomb;
self-storing in
handmade boxes.

Fuzzy Friends

Bear-with-Cub

Gund Anniversary Bear

Bear-with-Cub
5½ inches and 13 inches; plush; jointed limbs; swivel head; handmade by artist Elaine Fujita Gamble. Note wonderful facial expressions.

Fuzzy Felpa Hanger

Fuzzy Felpa

Gund Anniversary Bear
8 inches; plush; commemorating Gund's 85th year (1983); jointed limbs; swivel head; special tag.

Fuzzy Felpa
8 inches; mohair; Swiss; Felpa; jointed limbs; swivel head. Fuzzy-Hanger; 12 inches long; Felpa.

Janie Bear

Janie Bear
8¼ inches; mohair; handmade by artist Janie Comito; jointed limbs; swivel head; appealing. Also available through Christopher House Toys.

Baki Bear

Friendly Folk

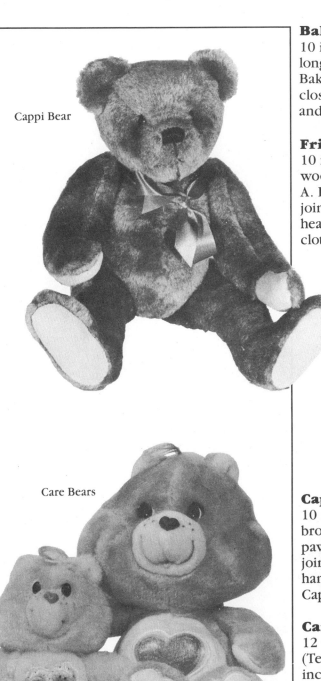

Cappi Bear

Care Bears

Baki Bear
10 inches;
long plush; German;
Baki; plastic nose;
close-set eyes; crown
and Berlin banner.

Friendly Folk
10 inches;
wool; handmade by
A. Bear and Friends;
jointed limbs; swivel
heads; handmade
clothes.

Cappi Bear
10 inches;
brown plush; tan
paws; glass eyes; fully
jointed; very special;
handmade by artist
Cappi M. Warnick.

Care Bears
12 inches
(Tenderheart) and 6
inches (Friend);
plush; motif on
stomachs; licensed
from American
Greetings
Corporation and
manufactured by
Kenner Products.

Eden's "Paddingtons" and
their "Aunt Lucy"

French Bear

German Hermann

Eden's "Paddingtons" and their "Aunt Lucy"
12 to 18 inches; plush; not jointed; dressed; Eden Toys, Inc.

French Bear
13 inches; luxurious plush; French; Skine (Jouets de Luxe), Paris; jointed limbs; swivel head; plastic nose; finest quality, as is companion cat, also Skine.

German Hermann
13 inches; German; Hermann; plush; plastic nose and safety eyes; not jointed; dressed.

Corduroy
14 inches; plush; dressed; storybook character (by Don Freeman); Trudy Toys Co., Inc.

Corduroy

Brown Bear

Jester

Time Machine Teddy

Terry Bear

Brown Bear

14 inches;
plush; felt paws;
jointed limbs; swivel
head; handmade by
artist Mary D. Olsen,
Graham Gridley Bear
Co.

Jester

15 inches;
jointed limbs;
beautiful satin, lace
jester suit; matching
cap; limited edition;
handmade by artists
Cheryl Lindsay and
Joanne Purpus.

Time Machine Teddy

15 inches;
mohair; shoe button
eyes; jointed limbs;
swivel head; hump;
musical; handmade
by artist Beverly Port;
irresistible.

Terry Bear

15 inches;
white plush;
flesh-colored suede
paws; shoe button
eyes; fully jointed;
extremely appealing;
handmade by artist
Terry Seim.

Strong Bears

Bully Bear

Strong Bears
16 inches and
12 inches;
mohair; German;
Steiff reproductions
of Margaret Strong
Museum bear; jointed
limbs; swivel heads.

Bully Bear
16 inches;
mohair; English;
made by House of
Nisbet, Ltd.; named
after bear expert
Peter Bull; jointed
limbs; swivel head.

Wright-hand Bear
17 inches; long gray
plush; jointed limbs;
swivel head;
handmade by artist
Beverly Wright.
Limited editions
available at Bears in
the Wood (see
Directory).

Rockwell Bear
17 inches;
wool and cotton;
English; Dean's
Childsplay Toys, Ltd.;
designed after bear in
a Norman Rockwell
painting.

Wright-hand Bear

Rockwell Bear

Chocolate Bear

Chocolate Bear
17 inches;
long plush; musical;
jointed limbs; swivel
head; handmade,
numbered and
registered by artist
Catherine Bordi; a
beautiful bear.

Peeking Panda

Fireman, save my bear!

Peeking Panda
17 inches; plush;
holds plastic bamboo
shoot; not jointed;
very cuddly; R. Dakin
& Company.

Fireman, save my bear!
18 inches;
plush; jointed limbs;
swivel head; "Cap'n
Smokey O'Bearin"
with rescued
cub-in-blanket; clever
design by Carrousel.

Bialosky Bears

Bialosky Bears
18 inches; plush; jointed limbs; swivel heads; reproductions of the bear from the cover of Workman Publishing's "The Teddy Bear Calendar"; made and dressed by Gund, Inc.

Merrythought Bear
19 inches; English; Merrythought, Ltd.; mohair; growler; jointed limbs; swivel head; "Edwardian Bear" limited edition of 1,000; signed and boxed.

Merrythought Bear

Toothy Teddy, two views

Lauren Bearcall

Toothy Teddy
19 inches;
shaggy plush; jointed
limbs; swivel head;
leather paws;
hand-sculpted mouth,
teeth, tongue and
claws; special edition
handmade by artist
Sarah McClellan (Sal's
Pals); truly unique.

Lauren Bearcall and Humphrey Beargart
20 inches;
fabric; not jointed;
Lauren wears hat
with veil and
imitation mink coat;
"Bogie," of course,
wears hat and trench
coat; both from North
American Bear Co.,
Inc.

Humphrey
Beargart

Floppy Bear

Floppy Bear

20 inches; German; Käthe Kruse; beige, woolly-looking plush; black button eyes and nose. Available in other colors.

King Ludwig

21 inches; plush, jointed limbs; splendid red velvet sewn-on suit; metallic gold trim; fur-trimmed crown; handmade by Ballard-Baines Bear Company.

King Ludwig

Beary Godmother

Beary Godmother
23 inches;
fluffy cream plush;
felt crown; satin
wings and wand;
metal spectacles; not
jointed; whimsical
and cuddly; by
Woods & Woods.

Thaddeus
26 inches;
shaggy plush;
internally jointed;
leather paws; from
Charleen Kinser
Designs.

Thaddeus

Bruino

Bruino

28 inches;
shaggy plush; jointed
limbs; swivel head;
suede paws; an
impressive fellow;
handmade by artist
Diane Babb.

Cub-and-Cat

Cub: 30 inches;
soft thick plush;
expressive face; not
jointed; "Classic
Teddy" and cat, both
by Avanti, Wallace
Berrie and Co., Inc. &
Jockline.

Cub-and-Cat

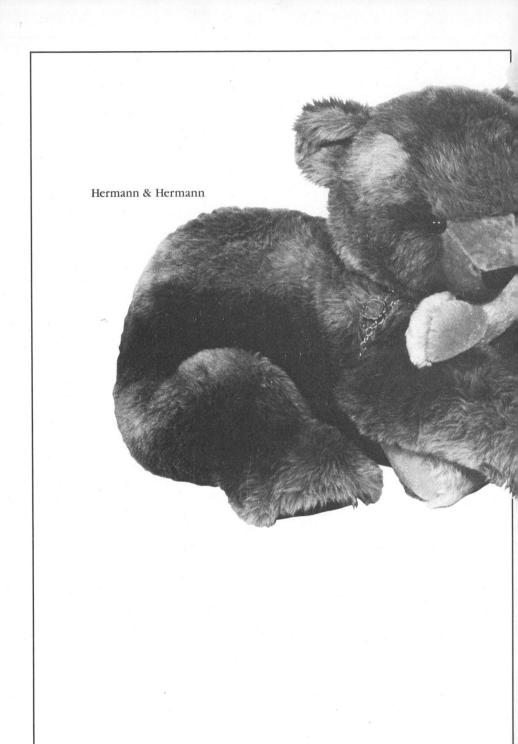

Hermann & Hermann

Hermann & Hermann
36 and 33 inches; one shaggy and sleepy; the smaller one is fully jointed; both large, quality pieces; German; Hermann.

Big Bear
41 inches; shaggy plush; jointed limbs; tail-moves-head mechanism (side to side); suede paws; musical; growler. Handmade by artist Beverly Port.

Big Bear

Big Things To Do With Little Bears

Miniature bears are usually thought of as those six inches high or less. The smaller they are, the more fun you can have displaying them.

Use props. Let these bears become incorporated into your favorite decor. If they are small enough, many Teddy Bears can be displayed in dollhouses or simply on dollhouse furniture—old or new. Because dollhouses are now important as collectibles, miniaturia, as the hobby is called, has produced an endless array of wonderful objects and habitats suitable for discriminating Teddy Bear owners.

Search dollhouse and craft shops for bargains. Houses come in conventional models as well as Victorian mansions. There are log cabins, townhouses, Cape Cods—you name it.

The most fun is finding treasures to put inside these houses. There is no limit. Any object you

German Wood Fort

have in your home or office is already available in miniature. Search them out at the miniaturia shows which are open to the public. Plus, if you are skilled at do-it-yourself projects, there are special tools and materials available, as well as kits of everyday items and even museum reproductions.

Miniaturia can be an overwhelming hobby with prices on tempting items running anywhere from a few cents for a little dinner plate to thousands of dollars for a pre-finished, lighted dollhouse. There is no need to spend a lot of money, though. You can have a great deal of fun using whatever you find around the house. The scenes pictured in these pages vary in decor from modern leftovers to museum-quality antiques. They all, however, have one major thing in common—they're innovative, comfortable and, in many cases, luxurious enough to allow your Teddy Bears to live in the style to which you yourself would like to be accustomed.

Miniaturia

German Wood Fort
27 x 21 x 19 inches; 1930s; buildings and bridges store in base compartment.

Red Double-deck Bus
23 x 12 x 7 inches; 1940s; steel; Scottish. Modern Steiff Teddy Bears and Pandas act as riders.

Red Double-deck Bus

Arm Chair

Dining Room Set

Old-Fashioned Band Concert

Arm Chair
Handmade English jointed bears (2½ inches and less) share a chair (inch-to-a-foot scale).

Dining Room Set
Old Steiff bears take tea.

Old-Fashioned Band Concert
Mini-musicians play in their own handmade wood bandstand.

Teddy Bear concert Tonite

Rugs and Pennants

Goebel Stuart Library

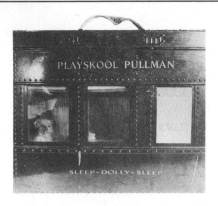 

Playskool Pullman Train Car, two views

Cabinet-Condo,
two views

Playskool Pullman Train Car

12 x 10 x 5 inches; early 1930s; tin; believed to be one of only one hundred ever produced; interior includes original curtains, pillows, sheets, blankets, table, berth, and closet.

Village Bakeshop, two views

Cabinet-Condo

Antique furniture, like this old dentist's cabinet, can be converted to comfortable bear-living; extra furniture is stored in drawers.

Village Bakeshop

14 x 10 x 11 inches; English wood "Jenny Wren" bakeshop has removable roof and enough handmade mini-treats for any bear in the bakery business.

Attentive Bear
(See page 95)

Directory

The following directory is a partial, yet representative listing of Teddy Bear manufacturers, importers, distributors, retail shops, artists, specialists, publications, and clubs. This is not intended to be a complete listing, but will be a helpful start for collectors.

Although it is not specifically mentioned, manufacturers, importers, and distributors listed usually carry Teddy Bears, other soft toys, or related items of interest. Additional information, when necessary, is described with some listings. Also, while most of the retail shops named are devoted greatly or exclusively to Teddy Bears, keep in mind that many major department stores have wonderful bear outpost-toy departments, too.

Listings in this directory should not be considered endorsements or recommendations by the authors or publisher of *The Teddy Bear Catalog.* Information was gathered from interviews, listings, and questionnaires, and although every effort has been made to make the information accurate and timely, the authors and publisher in no way can guarantee the companies or individuals appearing in the listings or be responsible for any related business transactions.

In contacting any of the companies and individuals listed *a self-addressed envelope with sufficient return postage must be enclosed.* Since some companies sell wholesale only, they may only be able to refer you to your nearest dealer.

This 1920s straw-stuffed Bandsman has brass buttons on his jacket and a removable hat.

Manufacturers, Importers, Distributors

A Bear and Friends
790 S.E. Webber, Suite 202
Portland, OR 97202
(503) 238-1278

Alresford Crafts, Ltd.
(Div. of Wallace Berrie)
3 Woodville Lane
Searingtown, NY 11507
(516) 621-3285

Animal Fair, Inc.
P.O. Box 1326
Minneapolis, MN 55440
(612) 831-7200

Applause
7628 Densmore
Van Nuys, CA 91406
(213) 787-2700
Applause, Avanti, Old Tyme Teddy

Art's Toy Manufacturing Co.
673 N. 13th
Easton, PA 18042
(215) 250-0888

Atlanta Novelty
(Div. of Gerber Products Co.)
47–34 33rd Street
Long Island City, NY 11101
(212) 392-8505

Ballard Baines Bear Co.
1826 114th N.E.
Bellevue, WA 98007
(206) 451-9322

Berg Plüschtierfabrik
A-6391
Fieberbrunn, Austria
05354-6236

Russ Berrie and Company, Inc.
111 Bauer Drive
Oakland, NJ 07436
(201) 891-7500
*Li'l Stuffies, Luv Pets, Luv Dolls, Puppet
Parade*

Canvas & Leather Bag Co., Inc.
132 RR Avenue
W. Haverstraw, NY 10933
(212) 549-8855
Teddy Bear tote bags, knapsacks

Carrousel
316 St. Nicholas Street
Midland, MI 48640
(517) 631-0209
*Sir Edward II, III, IV, others, costumed
bears*

Charm Company
713 South Claremont Street
San Mateo, CA 94402
(415) 344-7704, 348-6699

Classic Toys
318 W. 48th Street
Minneapolis, MN 55409
(612) 822-2079
*Alresford, Baki, Deans, Hermann, Käthe
Kruse*

**Commonwealth Toy & Novelty Co.,
Inc.**
27 West 23rd Street
New York, NY 10010
(212) 242-4070
*Executive Teddy Bear, Strawberry Bear,
others*

R. Dakin & Company
P.O. Box 7746
San Francisco, CA 94120
(415) 952-1777

Dallas Alice, Inc.
1047 Taft Street
Rockville, MD 20850
(301) 424-1640
*Teddy Bear silk-screened T-shirts,
sweatshirts, nightshirts*

Davis-Grabowski, Inc.
P.O. Box 381594
Miami, FL 33138
(305) 751-3667
Baki and Hermann, wholesale only

Dean's Childsplay Toys Ltd.
Pontnewynydd
Pontypool, Gwent, UK NP4 6YY
(04955) 4881
*Rockwell Bear, Porridge Bear, Dean's
Edwardian Bear, others*

Dollcraft Industries Ltd.
1107 Broadway
New York, NY 10010
(212) 807-7933

Dolls and Dreams, Inc.
19 West 24th Street
New York, NY 10010
(212) 689-3590
Dollsanddreams, Käthe Kruse

Eden Toys, Inc.
112 West 34th Street, Room 2208
New York, NY 10120
(212) 564-5980
Paddington

Etone International
112 Bay Street
Jersey City, NJ 07732
(201) 656-0480

Fagan International
1843 Business Center Drive
Duarte, CA 91010
(213) 286-7072
Hermann, Felpa, Käthe Kruse, Berg,
Original German Singing Bears, Reuge
Musical Bear, license plate holders,
bumper stickers, men's ties, other items

Freemountain Toys, Inc.
23 Main Street
Bristol, VT 05443
(802) 453-2462

Fun & Fancy Products
P.O. Box 188
Mill Valley, CA 94941
(415) 383-3030
Moon Bears

Furry Folk Puppets (Folkmanis,
Inc.)
1219 Park Avenue
Emeryville, CA 94608
(415) 658-7677
Bear puppets, other wildlife puppets

Goebel
Hummelwerk
250 Clearbrook Road
Elmsford, NY 10523
(914) 592-4050
Teddy Bear collectibles, accessories

The Grizzlies
Rt. 1, Box 410
Elberta, AL 36530
(205) 962-2500
New bears and kits to make them

Gund, Inc.
44 National Road
Edison, NJ 08817
Honey, Jolly, Snuffles, Bialosky, others

Gebr. Hermann KG.
Amlingstadter Str. 5
D-8606 Hirschaid, West Germany
(09543) 9161/9162

House of Nisbet Ltd.
Dunster Park Winscombe
Avon BS25 1AG England
(0934-84) 2905

Importoys, Inc.
P.O. Box 34488
Los Angeles, CA 90034
(213) 837-4477
Wholesale only

International Playthings, Inc.
151 Forest Street
Montclair, NJ 07042
(201) 783-7530
Anima, others

Jesco, Inc.
3250 Wilshire Boulevard, #1301
Los Angeles, CA 90010
(213) 381-3771
Hermann, P. & E. Rubin Sweet Line

Kenner Products
1014 Vine Street
Cincinnati, OH 45202
(513) 579-4000
Care Bears, Ewoks, other plush toys

Kingery Company
4318 4th Avenue N.E.
Seattle, WA 98105
(206) 632-9029
Jointed bears of wool and wool blends

Lenci Srl.
Via San Marino 56 Bis
Torino, Italy 10137
03911/323.960-399.676
Sales catalog

Marsh Division of Center Stage Housewares, Inc.
1224 East 28th Street
Los Angeles, CA 90011
(213) 232-1201
Teddy Bear serveware and kitchen accessories: Cookie jars, pitchers, more

Merrythought Limited
Iron Bridge, Telford
Shropshire, England TF8 7NJ
0952-45-3116

Mary Meyer Stuffed Toys
Mary Meyer Station
Townshend, VT 05353
(802) 365-7793
Mary Meyer and Linda Lee

Ms. Noah, Inc.
1106 Peake Street
Holly Hill, SC 29059
(803) 496-5473

North American Bear Co.
645 N. Michigan Avenue
Chicago, IL 60611
(312) 943-1055
Specific personalities and other costumed bears

Margot Owles, Imports from England
Box 135
Ewan, NJ 08025
(609) 478-4211
Cotton fabric printed with bear and doll patterns to cut out and make; Deans, Abydos Ltd.

Oxford Properties of California
3361 Oak Knoll Drive
Los Alamitos, CA 90720
(213) 594-0645
U.S. distributors of Little Folk, Canterbury Bears, Clancey Bears, Harrison Bears

Patmar Corporation
2300 Payne Avenue
Cleveland, OH 44114
(216) 566-9227

Projects International
5556 Francis Avenue
Chino, CA 91710
(714) 627-3691
Dean's Childsplay Ltd. bears and other items, Chinese bears

RamsHead Exclusives
3070 Kerner Boulevard
San Rafael, CA 94901
(415) 457-7180
Wool-stuffed sheepskin bears, other sheepskin toys

Reeves International, Inc.
1107 Broadway
New York, NY 10010
(212) 929-5412
U.S. representative of Margarete Steiff GmbH

Schmid
55 Pacella Park Drive
Randolph, MA 02368
(617) 961-3000
Bears and related items, Gordon Fraser giftware

Rollie Schmidt, Inc.
P.O. Box 3215
Toledo, OH 43607
(419) 531-0111
Mascots including Spoly, the Special Olympics Bear

B. Shackman & Co., Inc.
85 Fifth Avenue
New York, NY 10003
(212) 987-5162

Shirts Illustrated
1-B No. Salsipuedes Street
Santa Barbara, CA 93103
(805) 966-2222
Tiny Tees, Tee Team bears and puppets

Skine
20, Rue Carnot
95480 Pierrelaye, France
(3) 464 11 16
Skine, Vigand, Galic

Small World Toys
P.O. Box 5291
Beverly Hills, CA 90210
(213) 645-9680
Clemens German Teddy Bears

Philip Stahl, Inc.
Box 382
Pelham, NY 10803
(914) 738-0400/2222

Staufen Studio
8564 Mulberry Road
Chesterfield, OH 44026
(216) 729-7863
Teddy Bear clocks, ornaments, German imports

Margarete Steiff GmbH
P.O. Box 1560
D-7928 Giengen/Brenz, West Germany
07322-131-1

Suede-Craft Enterprises, Inc.
691 Executive Drive
Willowbrook, IL 60521
(312) 887-9895
Fuzzies flocked miniatures, jewelry and stationery items

Telemarks, Inc.
123 Main Street
Plaistow, NH 03865
(603) 382-8946
Mascot bears for schools, camps, and fund raising

Tide-Rider, Inc.
P.O. Box 9
Baldwin, NY 11510
(516) 223-3838, 3845
Merrythought, Lenci, House of Nisbet

Trudy Toys Co., Inc.
35 Lois Street
Norwalk, CT 06856
(203) 846-2005

Woods & Woods
725 Bryant Street
San Francisco, CA 94107
(415) 543-6058

Workman Publishing
1 West 39 Street
New York, NY 10018
(212) 398-9160

Retailers

Bazaar Des Bears
1927 First Avenue
Seattle, WA 98101
(206) 625-0596
New and antique bears, other antique toys, books

Bear Hugs—A Bear Emporium
7902 27th Street West
Tacoma, WA 98466
(206) 564-3700
New and antique bears, related items, newsletter

Bear-In-Mind, Inc.
73 Indian Pipe Lane
Concord, MA 01742
(617) 369-5987
Direct mail catalog of new bears and related items; also "The Arctophile," newsletter for collectors

Bear 'N Grin It
261 Del Amo Fashion Center
Torrence, CA 90503
(213) 54-BEARS
New bears, related items, handmade bears, including Linville Critters

The Bear Necessities, Inc.
Faneuil Hall Market Place
Boston, MA 02109
(617) 227-2327

26300 Cedar Road
Beachwood, OH 44122
(216) 464-6342

Westgate Mall
Fairview Park, OH 44126
(216) 356-2282

215 Goddard Row
Newport, RI 02840
(401) 849-9035

288A Thayer Street
Providence, RI 02840
(401) 351-3539
New bears, related items

Bear Street and the Pink Mushroom
415 West Foothill Boulevard
Claremont, CA 91711
(714) 625-2995

Bear To Bear
21217 Pacific Coast Highway
Malibu, CA 90265
(213) 456-9746
New bears, related items, handmade bears, kits, patterns, accessories

Bear Wares
60 Great Road, Rte. 2A
Acton, MA 01720
(617) 264-4560
*New bears, related items, handmade
bears, newsletter*

Bears, Etc.
93 Main Street
Cold Spring Harbor, NY 11731
(516) 367-9034
New bears, related items

Bears in the Wood
59 N. Santa Cruz Avenue
Los Gatos, CA 95030
(408) 354-6974
*Early all–Teddy Bear store, established
1976: new bears, related items,
handmade bears, other specialties*

Bears To Go
1400 Shattuck Avenue
Berkeley, CA 94709
(415) 644-BEAR
*New bears, related items, handmade
bears, bear repair, newsletter*

Beary Wonderful
*P.O. Box 8487
Santa Cruz, CA 95060
(408) 429-8323
New bears, related items, rubber stamps,
mail order*

Beauty & The Beast
835 N. Michigan Avenue
Chicago, IL 60611
(312) 944-7570

432 Robert Parker Road
Long Grove, IL 60047
(312) 634-6050
*New bears, related items, other new
plush toys*

Bell Enterprises
6921 Ridge Boulevard
Brooklyn, NY 11209
(212) 238-8042
*New and antique bears, other new plush
toys, mail order catalog*

B. N. Mail Order, Inc.
24 Union Wharf
Boston, MA 02109
(617) 542-8227
*Direct mail catalog of new bears and
related items*

**Bronner's Family Christmas
Wonderland**
25 Christmas Lane
Frankenmuth, MI 48734
(517) 652-9931
New bears, other new plush toys

Burton, Ltd.
475 Fifth Avenue, Room 203
New York, NY 10017
(212) 685-3760
Woven silk teddy bear ties, wallets

Virginia Caputo Antiques
1 Hawthorne Road
Holden, MA 01520
(617) 829-2686
*Antique bears, other antique toys, mail
order and antique shows only*

The Cat's Meow
4444 First Avenue N.E.
Cedar Rapids, IA 52402
(319) 393-6369
*New bears, related items, other new
plush toys*

Christopher House Toys
1800 4th Avenue
Seattle, WA 98101
(206) 292-9600

7010 35th Avenue N.E.
Seattle, WA 98115
(206) 523-9600
*New bears, related items, handmade
bears, other new plush toys, general line
of toys*

The Collectors Choice
10530 Metcalf
Overland Park, KS 66212
(913) 648-8000
*New bears, related items, handmade
bears, other antique toys*

Gene and Jo Sue Coppa
20 East Woodhaven Drive
Avon, CT 06001
(203) 673-3722
Antique bears, general antiques

B. Cornelius & Smith
137 Canal Square
Schenectady, NY 12305
(518) 372-0389
*New bears, related items, other new
plush toys, general toys*

Dollsville Dolls & Bearsville Bears
373 S. Palm Canyon Drive
Palm Springs, CA 92262
(619) 325-2241
New bears, handmade bears, related items, repair and bear-making supplies, antique dolls, mail order

Earth Bound
6314-B East Pacific Coast Highway
Long Beach, CA 90803
(213) 430-6239
New bears, handmade bears, related items, country items; woodland environment

The Enchanted Doll House
Route 7
Manchester Center, VT 05255
(802) 362-1327
New bears, related items, other new plush toys, dolls, miniatures, mini-workshop supplies, mail order catalog, newsletter

Enchanted Valley Doll Hospital & Bear Refuge
1700 McHenry Village Way
Modesto, CA 95350
1-800-TED-BEAR (Nationwide except California);
(209) 521-BEAR (California)
Antique and new bears, related items, repair, mail order, newsletter

Finch's Nest
2120 E. Moreland Boulevard
Waukesha, WI 53186
(414) 544-9010
Antique and new bears, related items, other plush toys

Franklin & Sons Wooden Soldier Toy Shops
4444 Robert Parker Coffin Road
Long Grove, IL 60047
(312) 634-3980

270 Market Square
Lake Forest, IL 60045
(312) 234-5991
New bears, related items, other new. stuffed toys

Gambucci, Our Own Hardware
1312 E. 13th Avenue
Hibbing, MN 55746
(218) 263-3480
New bears, other new plush toys

Georgetown Zoo
3222 M. Street N.W., #222
Washington, DC 20007
(202) 338-4182
New bears, other new plush toys

The Glass Rooster
P.O. Box 7001
Tacoma, WA 98407
(206) 752-7347
New bears, handmade bears, bear boxes, houses, and trunks

Good Hearted Bears
3 Pearl Street
Mystic, CT 06355
(203) 536-2468
New and antique bears, related items, handmade bears, heart-motif items

Grrreat Bears, Ltd.
301 South Light Street
Baltimore, MD 21202
(301) 244-8677
New bears, related items, handmade bears, other new plush toys

Hobbitat, Inc.
5717 Xerxes Avenue No.
Minneapolis, MN 55430
(612) 560-8188, 545-3616
Toys, new bears, related items, other plush toys

Hobby Center Toys
7856 Hill Avenue
Holland, OH 43528
(419) 865-5786
23 complete toy, bear, and doll stores in Ohio, Michigan, and Indiana

Hug A Bear
849 W. Harbor Drive
San Diego, CA 92101
(619) 230-1362, 326-6465

245 S. Palm Canyon Drive
Palm Springs, CA 92262
(619) 327-6465
New bears, related items, other new plush toys, mail order catalog, newsletter

Kelter–Malcé
361 Bleecker Street
New York, NY 10014
(212) 989-6760
Antique bears and general American antiques

The Land of Make Believe
134 N. Main Street
Hudson, OH 44236
(216) 650-4438
New bears, related items, other new plush toys, general gifts

Little Brown Bear
P.O. Box 42525
San Francisco, CA 94142
(415) 391-2342
New bears, other soft toys, mail order only

Louisiana Bear Company
6030 Line Avenue
Shreveport, LA 71106
(318) 865-7454
New bears, related items, other plush toys

Merrily Supply Co.
8542 Ranchito Avenue
Panorama City, CA 91402
(213) 894-0637
New bears, related items, supplies for making and repairing Teddy Bears, mail order catalog

My Little Red Wagon
120 E. Mill Street
Quaker Square, 3rd Level
Akron, OH 44308
(216) 384-1644
New bears, related items, other toys

My Sister and Me
1671 Penfield Road
Rochester, NY 14625
(716) 385-9322
New and antique bears, handmade bears, related items, repair, dolls, newsletter, mail order catalog

Nannies' Dolls & Miniatures
1235 Huntoon
Topeka, KS 66604
(912) 233-5591
New and antique bears and dolls, related items, other antique toys, repair

Nims Sportsmans of Ames
Box 150
Ames, Iowa 50010
(515) 232-4906
Toys, new bears, other plush toys

Oliver Enterprises
26 King's Road
Easterton, Wiltshire, England SN10 4PX
038081 2565
New bears, related items, other new plush toys, mail order only

Particularly Bears
Center Road, R.F.D. #1
Easton, CT 06612
(203) 261-4075
Antique and new bears, other antique toys

Paul's Pharmacy and Gifts—Teddy Bear & Collector's Corner
Sheridan Village
Bremerton, WA 98310
(206) 377-9202
New and antique bears, related items, other new plush toys, other antique toys, supplies for making bears

Playhouse Toys
(also **The Toy Maker**)
9433 Kirby Drive
Houston, TX 77054
(713) 799-8208
Twenty-two stores in Dallas and Houston with full line of quality toys and bears

Poppenhuis
Arubalaan 13
1213 Ve Hilversum, Holland
(035) 853669
Antique bears, related items, other antique toys, mail order

The Ready Teddy
Pier 39, #G-1
San Francisco, CA 94133
(415) 781-1255
New bears, related items, handmade bears, other new plush toys, mail order catalog, newsletter

Museum Gift Shop
Theodore Roosevelt Inaugural
Nat'l Historic Site
641 Delaware Avenue
Buffalo, NY 14202
(716) 884-0095
New bears, related items, other new
plush toys, newsletter

Bonnie Rowlands Antiques
531 E. Liberty Street
Medina, OH 44256
(216) 725-5982
Antique bears, toys, general antiques

Santa's Bear Shop
5300 Silver Springs Boulevard
Silver Springs, FL 32688
(904) 236-1200
New bears, related items, handmade
bears, other new plush toys, mail order
catalog

Saturday's Child, Ltd.
2146 N. Halsted Street
Chicago, IL 60614
(312) 525-TOYS
New bears, related items, other new
plush toys

Signature Collection
5–15 49th Avenue
Long Island City, NY 11101
(212) 361-1833
New bears, related items, mail order
catalog

Smith House—Bears & Antiques
3304 West Sixth Street
Topeka, KS 66606
(913) 357-0709, 272-1892
New bears, general and toy antiques

Stuffed Safari, Inc.
31065 Orchard Lake Road
Farmington Hills, MI 48018
(313) 855-6577
New bears, handmade bears, other new
plush toys, newsletter

Sugar Hill
P.O. Box 68
Novelty, Ohio 44072
(216) 338-5212
Antique bears, related items, shows only

Taylor's Toys
1025 Main
Great Bend, KS 67530
(316) 793-9698
New bears, related items, other new
plush toys, other antique toys

Ted E. Bears
1245 24th Avenue
San Francisco, CA 94122
(415) 665-7008
New bears, related items, Teddy Grams,
parties and balloons

Teddy Bear Country
108 W. Exchange Avenue
Fort Worth, TX 76106
(817) 624-7007
New, antique, and handmade bears;
country antiques

Teddy Bear's Picnic
1203 Lincoln Avenue
San Jose, CA 95125
(408) 292-8422
Antique, new, and handmade bears,
related items

Togram's Tidbits
P.O. Box 1093
Westford, MA 01886
(617) 251-8266
Bear related items: stationery, T-shirts,
books; mail order catalog

Toy Box Antiques
401 East Highway N.
Wentzville, MO 63385
(314) 327-8089
Antique bears, toys, general antiques

The Toy Shop (McFadden &
Associates, Inc.)
4710 B Interstate Drive
Cincinnati, OH 45246
(513) 874-4886
Stores in Cincinnati, OH, Indianapolis,
IN, Louisville, KY, Atlanta, GA.
New bears, related items, other new toys

Toys Ahoy!
28 Periwinkle Place
Sanibel Island, FL 33957
(813) 472-4800
New bears, related items, other new
plush toys

Toyworks, Inc.
3515 W. 69th Street
Minneapolis, MN 55435
(612) 822-8504

100 N. 6th Street
Minneapolis, MN 55403
*New bears, related items, handmade
bears, other toys*

Bunny Walker
P.O. Box 502
Bucyrus, OH 44820
(419) 562-8355
Antique bears, shows only

Wind Bells Cottage Antiques
720 Eighth Street
Hermosa Beach, CA 90254
(213) 374-1582
*New and antique bears, related items,
other antique toys, general antiques*

Winnie's Toy Orphanage
2401 Harding Road
Des Moines, IA 50310
(515) 277-6175
*New bears, related items, other plush
toys*

World of Toys & Hobbies
Conestoga Mall
Grand Island, NE 68801
(308) 384-5610
*New bears, related items, other new
plush toys, dolls, etc.*

Clubs

American Bear Club
Box 179
Huntington, NY 11743
(516) 271-8990

Good Bears of the World
P.O. Box 8236
Honolulu, HI 96815
(808) 946-2844

Invitational Bear Makers Guild
579 La Costa
Leucadia, CA 92024

**Northern California Teddy Bear
Boosters Club**
1203 Lincoln Avenue
San Jose, CA 95125
(408) 292-8422

Tacoma-Seattle Teddy Bear Club
P.O. Box 264
Graham, WA 98338
(206) 847-7224

Teddy Bear Boosters Club
P.O. Box 520
Stanton, CA 90680
(714) 827-0345

Teddy Bear Collectors Club
P.O. Box 601
Harbor City, CA 90710-0601

Twin Cities Teddy Bear Club
254 W. Sidney
St. Paul, MN 55107
(612) 291-7571

Bear Artists

Diane Babb (J. D. Babb, Inc.)
By Diane
1126 Ivon Avenue
Endicott, NY 13760
(607) 754-0391
*Teddy Bears and other plush animals,
kits, patterns, mail order catalog*

Catherine Bordi
The Chocolate Bear
P.O. Box 7501
Menlo Park, CA 94025
*Numbered, registered, and dated
handmade bears*

Regina Brock
Bearcrafts
2621 Brady Lake Road
Ravenna, OH 44266
(216) 296-4866
Miniature bears, bear art

Kit Chambers and Nick Cindric
American Folk Bear Company, Inc.
27787 Forestbrook
Farmington Hills, MI 48018
(313) 477-3160
*Jointed handmade bears, some limited
editions*

Janie Comito
My Bear
725 North 89th
Seattle, WA 98103
(206) 783-5811
Jointed handmade bears, repair

Joy Davis
Route 3, Box 164
Swanton, OH 43558
Jointed, handmade bears

Beth Garcia
25673 Flanders Drive
Carmel, CA 93923
(408) 624-5615
Fine jewelry and sculptured bear designs in gold, silver, ivory, bronze

Lori Gardiner
Echoes of the Past
30 S. First Avenue, Suite 181
Arcadia, CA 91006
(213) 447-1775
Jointed handmade bears, limited and special editions

Karen Haddon
The Strawberry Patch
142 Crestview Drive
Orinda, CA 94563
(415) 254-7842
Miniature plastic clay bear items

LaNore Kaplan
2983 Edgewood Road
Pepper Pike, OH 44124
(216) 831-1922
Jointed handmade bears

Maria Kwong Studio
Maria Kwong Bears, Bearware
3402 West Olympic Boulevard
Los Angeles, CA 90019
(213) 557-3483
Pins, necklaces, character bears, art pieces

Cheryl Lindsay and Joanne Purpus
Lindsay-Purpus Bears
1366 Eldean Lane
Oceanside, CA 92054
Limited edition handmade bears

Sarah McClellan
Sal's Pals
8622 E. Oak Street
Scottsdale, AZ 85257
(602) 941-8972
Jointed handmade bears, limited editions

Mary D. Olsen
Graham Gridley Bear Co.
P.O. Box 264
Graham, WA 98338
(206) 847-7224
Jointed handmade bears, patterns, repair

Sara Phillips
30 Locust Street, Apt. 2
Manchester, MD 21102
(301) 374-2115
Miniature jointed and dressed handmade bears

Beverly Port
Time Machine Teddies and Tinies
P.O. Box 711
Retsil, WA 98378
(206) 871-1633
Jointed handmade bears, dolls, related items

Kimberlee Port
Bitsy Bears
P.O. Box 632
Retsil, WA 98378
(206) 871-1633
Miniature jointed and dressed handmade bears, other plush toys

Terry Seim
Terry Bears
P.O. Box 7943
Federal Way, WA 98003
(206) 838-9035
Jointed handmade bears

Thomas Tear and Marcia Sibol
Bar Harbor Bear Co.
P.O. Box 498
Bear, Del 19701
Handmade bears and bear clothes

Veneta Smith
900 S. Rancho Avenue
Colton, CA 92324
(714) 825-5235
Handmade bears

Karen Walter
Old Time Teddy Bears
304 SE 87th Avenue
Portland, OR 97216
(503) 256-4563
Jointed handmade bears

Cappi M. Warnick
Bears by Cappi
940 Lance Avenue
Baltimore, MD 21221
(301) 687-6147
Jointed handmade bears, special editions

Carol-Lynn Rossel Waugh
5 Morrill Street
Winthrop, ME 04364
(207) 377-6769
Sculpted Teddy Bears in latex composition, watercolors of children and bears

Nancy Weik
Second Childhood Creations
Rt. 1, Box 60
Greenwood, WV 26360
(304) 659-2390
Handmade bears with removable costumes

April Whitcomb
April's Bears
3 Larkspur Way
Natick, MA 01760
(617) 653-0274
Miniature jointed sculpted bears, signed limited editions

Beverly Martin Wright
Wright Designs and Heirloom Bears (with Lynda Carswell)
890 Patrol Road
Woodside, CA 94062
Numbered and dated jointed handmade bears, limited editions

Bear Specialists

Bear University
302 S. Main Street
Albion, NY 14411
(716) 589-4363
Degrees awarded to bears, newsletter

Kay Bransky
R.D. #2, Box 558
Breinigsville, PA 18031
(215) 285-6180
Bear related items, mail order sales

Carol's Creations
1012 N. Summit, E
Iowa City, IA 52240
(319) 351-7854
Bear related needlework kits (counted cross stitch)

Tom Fletcher Bear Houses
1236 Lincoln Avenue
St. Paul, MN 55105
(612) 690-2707
Custom built bear houses and furniture

Frankies Designs
307 West Ave. A
Sweetwater, TX 79556
(915) 236-6050
Teddy Bear plaques, statues, and prints, numbered limited editions

Gadzooks Toys
Box 431
Hartford, VT 05047
(802) 295-5047
Zippered bear toys

Jerry Goldman
365 Edgewood Avenue
Teaneck, NJ 07666
(201) 833-1007
High-Bear-Nator bear-shaped beds

Hibearnations
Olde Brown Barn
Plympton, MA 02367
(617) 585-3483
Teddy bear photography and graphics

The Hugging Bear Inn & Shoppe
Main Street (Box 32), RR #1
Chester, VT 05143
(802) 875-2412
New bears, related items; bed and breakfast inn

Jeanne Miller
Miller's Bear Den
P.O. Box 111
Sherwood, OR 97140
Teddy Bear lecturer

S.S.F. Designs (Cracker Jill Jewelry)
4300 West Ohio Street
Chicago, IL 60624
(312) 722-8100
Teddy Bear jewelry made from original Cracker Jack prize molds

Teddy Bear Sandwich Den
3380 Barksdale Boulevard
Bossier City, LA 71112
(318) 747-7350
Restaurant with bears for decor and sale

Tiny Tocks
126 Susan Drive
Trenton, NJ 08638
(609) 882-3649
Teddy Bear clocks

Marlene Wendt
5935 Lyndale North
Brooklyn Center, MN 55430
(612) 561-6196
Teddy Bear rubber stamps, bear repair, handmade and antique bears

Publications

The Antique Trader Weekly and **The Antique Trader Price Guide to Antiques & Collectors Items**
The Babka Publishing Co.
P.O. Box 1050
Dubuque, IA 52001
(319) 588-2073

Antiques and The Arts Weekly
The Bee Publishing Company
5 Church Hill Road
Newtown, CT 06470
(203) 426-3141

Bear Tracks
Good Bears of the World
P.O. Box 8236
Honolulu, HI 96815
(808) 946-2844

The Grizzly Gazette
8622 E. Oak Street
Scottsdale, AZ 85257
(602) 941-8972

Hobbies, The Magazine for Collectors
1006 S. Michigan Avenue
Chicago, IL 60605
(312) 939-4767

Kovels on Antiques and Collectibles
Antiques, Inc.
P.O. Box 22200
Beachwood, OH 44122
(216) 831-5100

Long Island Heritage
29 Continental Place
Glen Cove, NY 11768
(516) 676-1200

Nutshell News Magazine
Clifton House
Clifton, VA 22024
(703) 830-1000

The Teddy Bear and Friends Magazine
Hobby House Press, Inc.
900 Frederick Street
Cumberland, MD 21502
(301) 759-3770

The Teddy Bear News
P.O. Box 8361
Prairie Village, KS 66208
(913) 642-0007

The Teddy Tribune
Barbara Wolters
254 W. Sidney
St. Paul, MN 55107
(612) 291-7571

Thumb Diddle "The Magic Bear"
Michael P.G.G. Randolph
P.O. Box 29818
Cincinnati, OH 45229
(513) 751-4809
Unique newsletter-with-extras for children

Tri-State Trader
Mayhill Publications, Inc.
P.O. Box 90
Knightstown, IN 46148
(317) 345-5133

Warman Publishing Co.
P.O. Box 26742
Elkins Park, PA 19117